I0820411

Praise for *How to Fall in Love with the Future*

'No one makes environmental optimism more credible or compelling than Rob Hopkins. Read this and don't weep.'

Hugh Fearnley-Whittingstall, chef and campaigner

'Rob Hopkins is one of the world's great optimists. He really believes that things can get better, and, when he's around, they usually do. This book will lift your spirits and give you hope.'

Brian Eno, musician, producer and artist

'This is exactly the book we need: it barges despair aside and reveals the many different and wonderful ways we could be.'

George Monbiot, *Guardian* columnist; author of *Regenesis*

'It's easy to know what we're fighting against: climate breakdown, social inequality and the destruction of nature. What's harder, and arguably more important, is to get clear on what we're fighting *for*. Rob has a gift of illuminating the better future that is possible and, critically, showing us where pockets of that future already live in the present. I shall carry around his latest book to ward off doom and despair and to remind myself of just what is possible when we allow ourselves to imagine.'

Clover Hogan, climate activist; founder, Force of Nature

'All successful movements for change have to have both light and shade, but the climate and nature movements have often focused much more on the shade – what we are losing and how painful that is. Without denying this reality, Rob Hopkins chooses to instead focus on the light – the compelling, intoxicating vision of what we can do if we get this right. This is a book that will regenerate your sense of possibility and purpose. An essential read.'

Tom Rivett-Carnac, political strategist, author and podcaster

'In this extraordinary work of imagination and storytelling, Rob Hopkins stunningly reveals the centrality of both creative acts for inventing utopian horizons. To arrive at the future in our dark times requires skilled guides who give us the space to think and feel what we never thought possible. No one is better at this task than Rob Hopkins. And this little book fires up the imagination in startling ways. You must read it.'

ALEX ZAMALIN, Rutgers University; author of *Black Utopia: The History of an Idea from Black Nationalism to Afrofuturism*

'Rob Hopkins invites us to fall in love with the future and demonstrates what a radical, transformative act this can be. At once visionary and deeply practical, Hopkins's new book sets out a route map to inspire change, unlock new possibilities and reignite activism.

'Urgent, powerful and exhilarating, *How to Fall in Love with the Future* shows us that the act of imagining a better future is the necessary first step towards achieving it – and that stories of real change happening right now provide compelling grounds for hope.'

CAROLINE LUCAS, former Green Party MP for Brighton Pavilion

'Playful and profound. This book brilliantly reveals how the imagination is our most underused resource for redesigning the future.'

ROMAN KRZNARIC, author of *The Good Ancestor* and *History for Tomorrow*

'I was a guest of Rob's on his podcast, talking about the power of sport in climate action, so I knew that Rob was a bit of a visionary; he just thinks differently and expresses himself wonderfully. This book is another fantastic example of that, enthusing his readers with the possibilities of a better tomorrow.'

DAVID GARRIDO, sports broadcaster and sustainability champion

'Rob Hopkins is a shining star in the firmament of generative thinking that will bring us all forward to a future we'd be proud to leave to the generations that come after us. If (when) we embrace the possibility of a flourishing world, Rob's waymarkers will have been key to us getting there. This is a clever, thoughtful, inspiring and beautiful book, and every single living human should read it.'

MANDA SCOTT, author of *Any Human Power*; co-creator, Thrutopia Masterclass

'Citizens everywhere are already creating a future worth falling in love with – it's just that the media radar is pointed in the wrong direction to see it. Rob doesn't just celebrate this very possibility – he helps us experience it through every sense we have. A vital contribution.'

Jon Alexander, co-founder, New Citizen Project; author of *Citizens: Why the Key to Fixing Everything is All of Us*

'If I say this book is delightful, do not think I mean frivolous. It is a stirring tribute to the potential of the imagination as a collective force for remaking the future. Lose yourself in these inspiring stories of activists, artists and educators worldwide who are tenderly cultivating new tomorrows and then look around you: you will see a more vivid, hopeful today. Hopkins not only makes complex ideas and difficult histories accessible and compelling; he also offers a rich bounty of examples and exercises for kindling the light of the radical imagination in these dark times.'

Max Haiven, PhD, Canada Research Chair in the Radical Imagination and associate professor, Lakehead University

'Imagine one of the kindest and brightest people in the world telling you how to shape the future into what you always dreamed of. That's what this book is about.'

Cyril Dion, writer, filmmaker and activist

'In a time when dark and self-serving forces are working to capture the future, we need a coordinated, global resistance of the imagination. Imagination – especially when practised together – is not a whimsical escape from reality but a vital force for reshaping it. As well as fighting the old, we must place our energy and attention on the futures we long for and tell stories about them as if they are already here. Rob's powerful and passionate book shares practical strategies on how to help people fall in love with these futures – and fight to make them real. Bold, hopeful and beautifully written, *How to Fall in Love with the Future* leaves you seeing the world through fresh eyes – and, most importantly, with your imagination fired up to create the world we'd be proud to leave for future generations.'

Phoebe Tickell, systems thinker and imagination activist; founder, Moral Imaginations

Also by Rob Hopkins

The Transition Handbook: From Oil Dependency to Local Resilience

The Transition Companion: Making Your Community More Resilient in Uncertain Times

The Power of Just Doing Stuff: How Local Action Can Change the World

21 Stories of Transition: How a Movement of Communities Is Coming Together to Reimagine and Rebuild our World

From What Is to What If: Unleashing the Power of Imagination to Create the Future We Want

How to Fall in Love with the Future

A Time Traveller's Guide to Changing the World

Rob Hopkins

Chelsea Green Publishing
White River Junction, Vermont, USA
London, UK

First published in 2025 by Chelsea Green Publishing | PO Box 4529 | White River Junction, VT 05001 | West Wing, Somerset House, Strand | London, WC2R 1LA, UK | www.chelseagreen.com
A Division of Rizzoli International Publications, Inc. | 49 West 27th Street | New York, NY 10001 | www.rizzoliusa.com

Publisher: Charles Miers
Deputy Publisher: Matthew Derr
Project Manager: Susan Pegg
Commissioning Editor: Muna Reyal
Developmental Editor: Brianne Goodspeed
Copy Editor: Susan Pegg
Proofreader: Sarah Greaney
Indexer: Charmian Parkin
Designer: Abrah Griggs

ISBN 978-1-915294-51-7 (hardcover) | ISBN 978-1-915294-53-1 (UK ebook) | ISBN 978-1-64502-366-1 (ebook) | ISBN 978-1-915294-54-8 (audiobook)
Library of Congress Control Number: 2025010153 (print)
A CIP catalogue record for this book is available from the British Library.

Our Commitment to Green Publishing
Chelsea Green sees publishing as a tool for cultural change and ecological stewardship. We strive to align our book manufacturing practices with our editorial mission and to reduce the impact of our business enterprise in the environment. We print our books on chlorine-free recycled paper, using vegetable-based inks whenever possible. This book may cost slightly more because it was printed on paper that contains recycled fiber, and we hope you'll agree that it's worth it. *How to Fall in Love with the Future* was printed on paper supplied by Sheridan that is made of recycled materials and other controlled sources.

Authorized EU representative for product safety and compliance
Mondadori Libri S.p.A. | www.mondadori.it
via Gian Battista Vico 42 | Milan, Italy 20123

Printed in the United States of America.
10 9 8 7 6 5 4 3 2 1 25 26 27 28 29

Contents

'The future is obvious, but the potential impossible is calling softly and knocking gently.'

Sun Ra

To Emma, Rowan, Finn, Arlo and Cian.

To Katie, Bex and Grace.

To Mum, Tessa, Jo, Iun, Jake and Archie.

To the vibrant and flourishing
free Palestine of the near future.

And in memory of
Marina O'Connell and Dr Stephan Harding.

Introduction

Travelling through time was disorientating the first few times I did it, but I feel as though I've got the hang of it now. Just as sailors get their 'sea legs', I've got my 'time legs'. There is a beautiful phenomenon you notice as a time traveller: once you start to accelerate, once the years really start to fly past, you see a kind of rainbow halo effect through the portholes, a shimmering mirage that causes you to pause in the delicate calibration of your Disbelief Suspenders and take a moment to just absorb the majesty. It's a bit like the Northern Lights, but in the full spectrum of colours. I'd love to show you one day.

I'm travelling with my friend and colleague, Mr Kit, on one of our expeditions to document the future. As we approach 2030 and begin to decelerate and descend, I get goosebumps, a nervous frisson as we touch down.[1] There are, of course, an infinite number of possible futures that lie ahead of us, quantum threads stretching out into the distance. We have explored many of them, including some of the nightmare scenarios and, believe me, you don't want to go there.

However, since Mr Kit and I perfected the design of our Cynicism Overrider Circuits a couple of months back, we've been able to follow the quantum threads to a 2030 that resulted from humans doing everything we could have possibly done to avert climate disaster. It's no utopia, but it's no dystopia either. It's a work in progress. But, damn – it's an amazing work in progress.

After Mr Kit and I land, I pop open the hatch and we step out. We've grown quite good at finding discreet places to land so that nobody really notices us arrive and depart. This time, we are on a residential city street, pretty average in a lot of ways, and yet its transformation in recent years has been remarkable. Right away, I notice that the air smells much cleaner than what we were breathing back in the present. I know by now that this is because there are far fewer cars on the roads, that fossil fuels have been phased out and that efforts have been made to reduce air, water and ground pollution. The result is an atmosphere that smells like the first evening when spring begins to turn towards summer – but also somewhat more complex than that.

Indeed, it's hard to disentangle the different scents and smells that combine to create the rich aroma of the future. In the way a sommelier may savour a complex wine, I inhale deeply and attempt to identify the different nuances and aromas. I recognise thyme, lavender and a Caribbean herb known as broadleaf thyme or Spanish oregano. The air smells like growing things. It smells like honey, like damp earth, like a forest. It smells of good food cooking. It smells like flowers, intoxicating and delicious.

The second thing I notice after we step into 2030 is the birdsong. It's louder than what we left behind but also richer. At first, I am disorientated by it. There are birds whose serenades I don't even recognise. In 2030, prizes are awarded to urban communities for the diversity and complexity of their birdsong so that the residents of various neighbourhoods engage in good-natured competition to build and erect bird boxes, plant trees, shrubs and wildflowers, and leave leaf litter on the ground to create habitats for the insects that birds like to eat. The ban on pesticides and herbicides didn't hurt, either.

Some neighbourhoods have become known for particular species of birds, and at certain times of year people will travel across the city just to listen. Many residents now use songbirds as their wake-up call, something only possible because of how much louder they are now than they once were. This place feels more like an aviary with buildings in it than an actual city. Groups of nighttime revellers will sometimes end the evening by heading to a particular neighbourhood where the nightingales have returned, to bathe in the birds' melodious song.[2]

Thanks to the fact that there are significantly fewer cars on the roads, the score of our lives is no longer set to the constant hum of the internal combustion engine but rather to the sounds and symphonies that emerge from nature. Mr Kit and I are hearing the world around us in greater subtlety and detail, a richer granularity. I also notice more laughter than I did in the world I left behind, and the sounds of rambunctious children from every direction.

As we walk around, I see a different look in people's eyes. People hold us in friendly and curious eye contact as they pass. It could be, of course, that they are fascinated by our time travellers' costumes, white all-in-one suits, designed not to protect us but to protect them from the present-day despondency we may have accidentally brought with us. (We learned in Time Traveller Training that pastsplaining – saying things like 'that's never going to work' – is forbidden.) But there's more to it than that. There is a sense of shared excitement on the streets. It's a feeling of 'we might just do this' that was mostly missing on the streets that Mr Kit and I just left.

A lot of the anxiety, tension and despair we felt back in the present seems to have dissipated here. People feel part of a historic shift happening around them. They have discovered that when you find yourself doing something you love, you have more energy, determination and clarity than you could have ever imagined. People are acting like they are part of a team. They seem less guarded, less hurried, less urgent, more open. The word that keeps coming into my mind is 'dignity'. People

The Five Rules of Time Travelling

1. **No bringing any books back.** That's cheating. People in the present have to figure this out on their own.
2. **Avoid the silly stuff.** You know, killing your grandparents or falling in love with your mother, that kind of thing. It creates a mess that's very hard to unpick.
3. **No pastsplaining.** As sociologist Ruha Benjamin puts it, 'We need to give the voice of the cynical, skeptical grouch that patrols the borders of our imagination a rest.'[3]
4. **Make sure your batteries are fully charged before setting off.** You don't want to go all that way only for your recording devices to run out of charge.
5. **Never time travel for personal gain.** Intention and motivation are all-important. Travel for curiosity and for the wellbeing of others.

here are moving with a greater sense of self-belief. It feels like life – all life – is thriving.

You see, this place I'm visiting, this future, is several years into a Marshall Plan-scale response to the current climate and ecological emergency.[4] Political ambition, resources and collective imagination have all been harnessed for a profound reconception of how society functions. Sure, there were people who said it wasn't possible, that it would be too expensive, that maybe we should move more slowly, that we needed to wait until we had it all figured out before we set sail, but nobody remembers those people anymore, just like nobody remembers the people who criticised suffragettes over a century ago for being unrealistic and hysterical. As physical health, mental health and biodiversity rebounded, a collective sense of excitement and shared purpose rebounded along with it.

Climate change hasn't disappeared. The world is still warming, but it's on the slowest trajectory possible because we all did everything we could possibly have done to avert disaster. We took all possible measures to prepare for climate chaos, combined with all possible measures to draw down carbon. The stories Mr Kit and I see on newsstands as we walk by describe and celebrate ocean kelp forests ('seaforestation'), reforestation of the Amazon, restoration of peatlands and the rebuilding of soils around the world.

Looking around, I'm struck by how much softer the city feels. Less tidy. Less regimented. Messier, but in a good way. Freer, like you might feel when you're finally able to kick off a pair of shoes that are too tight. This is at least partly because of the depaving projects that accelerated after several hot summers impressed upon city planners that concrete and tarmac are dangerous at high temperatures; hardscapes hold heat, everyone now knows, rather than enabling cities to cool.

About 40 per cent of the city's hard surfaces have now been depaved, resulting in a cooler, softer, more porous feeling to the landscape. As one depaver reports, 'It feels like you're liberating soil.'[5] Playgrounds, car parks, and areas around offices and shopping centres have been depaved and turned into havens for wildlife.[6] The trend of paving over front gardens now runs in reverse, assisted by depaving grants for city residents, so front garden spaces are instead filled with flowers and mini-rewilding experiments.

We see newly planted trees everywhere, tended by people living close to them, in an effort to create a tree canopy across all areas of the city. This cultivation of an urban forest reduced crime and fostered a greater sense of community, as people began leaving their homes more to enjoy the shade, take part in outdoor activities, meet friends, play chess, and dug out their old sketchbooks and coloured pencils to enjoy drawing in the dappled light.[7] The impacts of this initiative, mostly led by citizens, exceeded everyone's expectations.

Mr Kit points out staircases on the sides of buildings that have been decorated by street artists with paintings of climbing plants. These staircases invite us to enter a different realm of the city: its rooftop world. As we reach the top steps, we emerge into a verdant panorama of trees, gardens and recreational spaces. We see a morning yoga class on one rooftop, beehives on another and a patchwork of different-coloured salads growing on several others.

This green realm stretches out beyond the roof of the building we're on. Most of the roofs are connected by walkways and bridges wide enough that people bring their bicycles up and cycle from rooftop to rooftop. A few years ago, the city government implemented new policies that supported the construction of such walkways and bridges.[8]

Many of the larger roofs have been turned entirely into gardens, and we see teams of people working on them. Some of these rooftop gardens are commercial operations, producing the freshest food in the city, marketed as 'food feet, not food miles'. The gardens are also living sponges, absorbing and storing rainwater and reducing the surge of water off roofs during storms, thereby reducing flooding and erosion on the land below.[9] Of course, the depaving projects have also helped the city's soils absorb more water, resulting in less damage, more carbon capture, greater biodiversity and healthier microclimates.

From this height, Mr Kit and I gaze across the city to the land beyond, which also looks different than it once did – less tidy, more diverse, more forested. Two women are sitting together at a cafe table taking in the view as well. We introduce ourselves and learn that the friends, Sally and Fatima, spend a lot of time up here. They've never met time travellers, though, they laugh. They are both in their mid-20s, and their effortless blending of fashion from the 1950s, 1970s and 2000s is quirky and cool. We're fascinated to hear them describe how the world made it to this point. What Mr Kit and I want to know is the sequence, the cascade of events that produced this future?

'I'm always struck,' Sally tells us, 'when I rewatch old TV shows, how being cynical was normal and cool. It wasted so much energy! But a movement began to grow that saw cynicism as undesirable, something that robbed us of energy and possibilities. I look back and I'm so glad those days of cynicism are behind us. I feel like we were part of the generation that had to decide: we can be cynical or we can try to solve problems. So, we became the generation that realised our future depended on each other, and that became our guiding star.'

'It was a very close-run thing,' Fatima says, her voice cracking for a moment, as she describes the world they left behind. 'The worst-case scenarios were coming true. But we saw this incredible movement emerge. Millions of young people began to demonstrate. They glued themselves to oil company offices and the banks that invested in them, disrupted their meetings, drew attention to the cause. There were many thousands of arrests. People even died for it.[10] Governments enacted laws to try to silence the protesters. But public awareness began to shift, and once that started, things began to change with astonishing velocity.

'There were also legal cases that curtailed the power of the oil and gas industry, and forced governments to decarbonise more ambitiously. One catalyst was an obscure US federal law related to civil asset forfeiture that enabled law enforcement to seize property from criminals. Believe it or not, this precipitated the downfall of the fossil fuel industry.[11] Civil asset forfeiture doesn't require a conviction or even an arrest, just reasonable grounds that the asset in question is linked to alleged criminal activity.

First in the United States, and then around the world, legal cases established that oil and gas companies were engaged in criminal activity, which led to the seizure, nationalisation and dismantling of oil company assets. Once that happened successfully, similar legal tools were also applied to gain similar ground.[12]

'We realised we were part of the biggest movement in history, the movement to save civilisation. It aligned in a way no one could have anticipated.' Fatima pauses to wipe away a tear. 'It was amazing.' She sighs, looking out towards the horizon.

I ask Fatima what if felt like to be part of that movement, and she takes a moment to reflect. 'I think activism became much more emotionally smart,' she begins. 'We realised that our own emotional needs, which consciously or unconsciously we bring to our activism, like our need to be right, our need to gain status for what we do, our need to make ourselves feel better and our need to show how wrong our opponents are, didn't necessarily help. We recognised our own inclinations towards burnout. We recognised that the potential to control and dominate is present in all of us. Now we support each other better. We stand *for* something, not just in opposition. People speak to each other across political divides in a way that builds common ground. We also got better at storytelling, which ignited the longing for a better world.

'This world is not a utopia by any means,' Fatima continues. 'We all know this is just the start of a process. But we believe today, as we did not back then, that many more people will survive if we take ambitious steps. Look around you: it's amazing. We already get 80 per cent of energy from renewables and scientists tell us that those worst-case scenarios we were so terrified of have been avoided. We very narrowly averted catastrophe through a response rooted in compassion.' Fatima pauses to take a deep breath.

Sally picks up the thread. 'When I look back, I remember the hardest thing was getting started. It felt like an unscalable mountain. But once we were on the mountain, and working as a team, it became much clearer. Human beings turned out to be infinitely more adaptable and resourceful than we imagined we were. So many of the changes we've seen are beyond what I thought people were capable of in such a short period of time.'

Fatima goes on to tell us how community, and the commons, became the central organising principle of society. People lost respect for wealth. It became seen as a systemic kink that some people could become hugely rich, while others grew impoverished. There was a new shared disdain for massive wealth: it was seen as deeply unattractive. It showed a lack of something, not the presence of something.

Fatima points out across the city. 'So much of what you see down there is now community owned,' she says. 'It's a commons. It's underpinned by a change in culture. We consume less, but people have more time for connection, caring, comedy, crafting, community, creativity, all the things that make us feel good. I would say that this is a time of cautious optimism.'

'Cautious optimism'. Fatima's words stay with me as Mr Kit and I thank her and Sally for their time, before heading down the steps and back into the city. One of the shifts that seems to have shaped this future was the move in 2027 away from Gross Domestic Product (GDP) as a measure of progress. It was decided that GDP measures all the wrong things. The fact that something is larger than it was the previous year is no indication of whether it's any better or not. We now measure the things that matter, like the number of kids playing in the streets, the percentage of people with healthy teeth, the number of women able to cycle home alone after dark, attention span, and time spent outdoors.

So many people back in the present day told me this future was impossible, that this world could never become a reality.

But it can become reality. I've seen it. And I hope you will pause for a moment to suspend your disbelief and see it too.

◆ ◆ ◆

Back in 2020, when the Covid-19 pandemic landed on our doorsteps and disrupted every aspect of daily life, I responded the way a lot of people did: by starting a podcast. My podcast was called *From What If to What Next*, and each episode featured two guests. Rather than a deep dive into a given subject, my guests and I would start by time travelling together to 2030. We would walk together down imagined streets, exploring the future world with all our senses.

The fictional journey that (my very real friend) Mr Kit and I took to 2030 is built from descriptions my podcast guests shared with me. My guests have been economists, community organisers, academics, Indigenous activists, mycologists, poets, entrepreneurs, politicians, psychologists, futurists, fashion designers, mental health campaigners, theatre producers, bakers, comedians, advertising executives, novelists, Afrofuturists, curators, Olympians, prison abolitionists, sports reporters, ecologists and more. What they all share in common is a willingness to suspend their disbelief long enough to imagine, and then describe, a future they would actually want to live in.

From the podcast's inception, I set myself one ground rule: I would never do a single episode with two white men as guests. It was a resolution that required considerable determination at times because many organisations, when asked to recommend someone as a guest, will push a white guy to the front. But with the help of organisations like Climate Reframe, which supports Black, Brown, Asian, people of colour and UK-based Indigenous peoples from the Global South in their climate work, it turned out to be one of the most rewarding challenges I've ever set myself.[13]

Why? Well, for a lot of reasons, but chief among them was my discovery that some of the most interesting work being done right now on the impoverishment of our collective imagination at this crucial moment in history and what we might do about it is being done by Black women, Indigenous rights activists, and queer and non-binary people. And the more podcast episodes I did, and the more people I spoke with, the more I began to rethink the work I had been doing for decades.[14] I'll introduce you to some of the people whose work inspired me the most as we travel through this book.

I want to take you on a journey, with the help of my time machine, into a way of creating change in the world that will probably be different than what you're used to. I don't claim to have all the answers. It's more of a feeling that has grown within me, as I've worked with different people and taken part in the activities and exercises that I'll share with you in this book, that there is a different approach to activism that could unlock some very different possibilities and scenarios. I want this book to inspire you not to think that Mr Kit and I are time travellers but rather that we can *all* be time travellers, and by taking a more fluid and playful approach to time, by creating lived experiences of a future resulting from our doing everything we could possibly have done, we can map out a route to inspire change. You may, at this point, be thinking that time travel is impossible, but by the end of this book, I hope I will have moved you to a position of feeling exhilarated about the possibilities it brings.

PART ONE

Why Build a Time Machine?

CHAPTER ONE

The Situation Is Urgent

In May 2024, the *Guardian* surveyed 380 climate scientists from around the world about the climate crisis and humanity's potential to avert it. Of these scientists, 77 per cent responded that they believe global temperatures will reach at least 2.5°C above pre-industrial levels: a catastrophic level of heating. Furthermore, 42 per cent responded that they believe global temperatures will even exceed 3°C. Only 6 per cent of the scientists surveyed think we will succeed in limiting global temperatures to the 1.5°C increase established by the 2015 Paris Agreement on climate change.

Dr Ruth Cerezo-Mota, an expert in climate modelling at the National Autonomous University of Mexico, told the *Guardian* that following the many recent climate-change-related natural disasters worldwide, she thought governments would finally act. However, she remarked, 'I think 3°C is being hopeful and conservative. 1.5°C is already bad, but I don't think there is any way we are going to stick to that. There is not any clear sign from any government that we are actually going to stay under 1.5°C . . . Sometimes it is almost impossible not to feel hopeless and broken.'[1]

I know how she feels. I've been involved in climate activism for more than twenty years and have had many such moments of feeling hopeless and broken myself. As I often say to audiences, if you're not regularly terrified about climate change, you're not paying attention.

There are good reasons for feeling broken and hopeless. In its *Emissions Gap Report 2022*, the United Nations declared that it's still possible to avoid runaway climate change but that 'wide-ranging, large-scale, rapid and systemic transformation is now essential'.[2] That means that rather than pretending the climate crisis will disappear with a few feel-good tweaks to public policy or consumer behaviour, we need to dramatically reduce our CO_2 output from the current UK average of 7.6 tonnes per person per year to 2.3 tonnes by 2030, 1.4 tonnes by 2040 and 0.7 tonnes by 2050.[3] That's huge.

And we don't have long to do it. In other words, climate change is a crisis that demands we change pretty much everything – and fast.

What would it look like, I asked Dr Peter Kalmus, a climate scientist at NASA's Jet Propulsion Laboratory, if we were to change everything in accordance with what climate scientists are telling us? What does 'wide-ranging, large-scale, rapid and systemic transformation' actually look like in practice?

Dr Kalmus told me that for some things it's too late; humanity has already caused losses we are unable to reverse. But to preserve what we still can would require that every nation go into what Kalmus calls 'emergency mode'.

According to Dr Kalmus, emergency mode means building out renewables as quickly as possible and ending the extraction, selling and burning of fossil fuels within five years. We'd need to nationalise the oil and gas sector and end industrial animal agriculture, especially beef. These two things – an end to fossil fuels and an end to industrial animal agriculture – are what he calls 'the bottom line'. These are the non-negotiables. But, Dr Kalmus says, we'd also need to share wealth far more equally, both from rich nations to poorer nations and from the billionaire and multimillionaire class to the working class.

Assuming we did all those things – admittedly on the outer edges of possibility but possible nonetheless – I asked him what might we hope for?

'*If* we go into emergency mode now,' Dr Kalmus told me, 'we do, I think, probably stay well under 2°C of global heating. I don't think most people understand how precious every fraction of a degree is right now, for humanity and for life on Earth.'

In this scenario, Kalmus says, temperatures would start to come back down again around the end of this century, peaking around 2080 before beginning to decline. The implementation of natural approaches to sequestering carbon, such as rewilding, rebuilding soils, developing aquatic kelp forests and planting trees, could help speed things up.[4]

This is not merely an academic exercise for Peter Kalmus. Faced with an insider's knowledge of how grave our situation is, he gave up flying, eating meat and using fossil-fuelled vehicles, cutting his own carbon footprint by 90 per cent. In April 2022, he was arrested in Los Angeles for chaining himself to a Chase Bank building in protest of the company's continued investment in fossil fuels. In November 2022, Dr Kalmus was again arrested on trespassing charges for protesting at a private jet terminal in Charlotte, North Carolina. In 2023, he moved his family away from Altadena in Los Angeles, fearing that the hotter and drier summers would at some point lead to fires in the area. Two years later, from their new home in North Carolina, his family watched their former home and neighbourhood burn to the ground on TV.[5]

Kalmus told the *New York Times*, 'Five years ago, the majority view was that it was unacceptable to be an activist and to speak out if you were a scientist. I think the majority view now is you probably should be doing that because the science is so frightening.'[6]

Kalmus is not alone in his feeling that desperate times call for desperate measures. And some of these measures have been effective – to a degree. For example, Insulate Britain ran non-violent disruptive actions on motorways across the UK to raise awareness of the need to insulate the nation's housing. This resulted in increased coverage of the issue in the media and Parliament, had a positive effect on other organisations already working to promote home insulation and, in less than a year, helped prompt a £1 billion government investment known as the Great British Insulation Scheme. While public opinion was generally negative about Insulate Britain's approach and tactics, support for the message itself was consistently favourable.[7]

Likewise, Extinction Rebellion has successfully raised the profile of the climate emergency, the need to tell the truth about it, and the risk of extinction and Earth-systems breakdown. Extinction Rebellion shifted the Overton window to a public discourse that recognised the urgency of the situation; local authorities and other organisations declared a climate emergency following Extinction Rebellion's occupation of sites across London in April 2019.

School strikes, such as the youth-led Fridays for Future, which began in 2018 with Greta Thunberg protesting outside Sweden's Parliament every Friday – lasting, all told, for 251 weeks – have also had their impact. These strikes mobilised hundreds of thousands of young people, raised awareness of climate change – especially its impact on young and marginalised people around the world – and led to a decline in consumer behaviours such as eating meat and flying. In Sweden alone, there was a 9 per cent decline in flying between 2018 and 2019, due to what became known as 'the Greta effect'.[8]

Fridays for Future strikes have been noted, in particular, for the empowering effect they've had on young women and girls, a demographic still under-represented in politics but who became the movement's most prominent figures.[9] The strikes also influenced the German Federal Constitutional Court's

2021 ruling that Germany's climate policies were not sufficiently ambitious.[10]

Perhaps even more than reducing parts per million of carbon in the atmosphere, Peter Kalmus told me that activism helps 'in terms of our collective mindset, that we start to see ourselves as caretakers and not as extractors, that you can't consume your way out of unhappiness'.

All around us, we can see the clear signs that things are not going well. Humanity is in the midst of a huge, overarching, interconnected existential crisis; one we are failing to successfully address. Biodiversity is plummeting, the impacts of the climate emergency are unfolding faster than scientists predicted and yet governments, and other institutions like banks, are rolling back on actions to respond to it.[11] It's a crisis with its roots in the extractivist belief that the natural world and the world's poorest people exist to be exploited by the world's wealthiest nations, that economies can grow infinitely, and that we should have little concern for the impacts generated by the way we live our lives. Its most obvious manifestation is the climate and ecological emergency. But it's not the only manifestation.

Research shows a correlation between pollution and poor mental health, and the rapid, unpredictable and often terrifying changes caused by climate uncertainty and instability can prompt feelings of helplessness, grief, despair and fear.[12] Levels of sewage in British rivers are, at the time of writing, so high that the 2024 Oxford–Cambridge Boat Race organisers instructed rowers to not enter the River Thames due to high levels of E. coli, which sickened numerous Oxford rowers during training. Leonard Jenkins, a rower on the Oxford team, told the BBC, in a way that seemed to sum up the national mood, 'It would be a lot nicer if there wasn't as much poo in the water.'[13]

Researchers have studied some of these impacts on young people, coining terms such as 'climate-change anxiety', 'solastalgia', 'eco-anxiety', 'ecological grief' and 'climate-related psychological distress' to describe what they see.[14] Between 1990 and 2019, depression, self-harm, anxiety and schizophrenia increased substantially among those between the ages of twenty-five and seventy-four.[15] The World Health Organization (WHO) has shown that in 2010, anxiety and depression, the two most-commonly observed mental disorders, led to a $1 trillion decline in global GDP, and that lost output due to mental, neurological and substance-abuse disorders resulted in a loss to the global economy of between $2.5–$8.5 trillion, a figure the WHO anticipates will double by 2030.[16]

In 2023, Oxfam reported that of the $42 trillion of new wealth created since 2020, the richest 1 per cent enjoyed two thirds, which is twice as much as the bottom 99 per cent has combined.[17] Ironically, it is the 1 per cent who are disproportionately responsible for the climate emergency. In 2019, the wealthiest 1 per cent were responsible for more CO_2 emissions than the poorest 66 per cent – more than five billion people.[18]

Besides the growing understanding that things are going very badly indeed, many people, thankfully, seem to be reaching the conclusion that just talking about what is broken is no longer enough – if it ever was. Yet when we step up to try to shift the massive and complex system that is driving this mess, even our most dedicated efforts seem to be falling short. In my hometown of Totnes, Devon, often held up as the poster child of community-led responses to the climate and ecological emergency, a town where a committed group of activists have dedicated their lives to pre-emptively creating a post-carbon future for almost twenty years now, we are forced to confront the fact that, despite all our efforts, we've failed to slow this monster down.

I co-founded the Transition movement in 2006 as a community-led behaviour change model that empowers citizens to reimagine and rebuild every aspect of their hometowns – from the local economy and transportation to the food system.[19] Transition has since spread to fifty countries with many incredible stories of success. And yet, since its founding, humanity has poured CO_2 into the atmosphere in ever-increasing quantities.

'My fondest wish is to, before I die,' Kalmus told me during our conversation, 'feel like humanity has made that shift. Has turned that corner. And maybe by the time I die, things won't be in the process of cooling down yet, but in terms of humanity's path forward, I just want to feel like we've shifted somehow into that world of mutual aid and sharing and being good planetary roommates. Is it too much to ask?'

No, I don't think it is. Peter Kalmus's vulnerability and willingness to put himself out there as a scientist made me wonder if maybe we should be doing the same things as activists. And so, I have a question for you. What if the role of activism – in addition to raising awareness and pointing out the dangers of particular policy decisions and so on – was to mobilise, on a previously unimaginable scale, a deep and intense longing for a different future? What would we do differently? What would that activism look like? What skills might we need that we currently don't have? More and more people are asking these questions.

Paul Goodenough, for example, is the founder and CEO of an organisation called Rewriting Earth, a collaboration of more than three hundred of the world's best storytellers, including writer Alan Moore, actor and model Cara Delevingne, and writer, director and actor Taika Waititi, who are weaving new stories about our relationship with the natural world. Speaking on the *Outrage and Optimism* podcast in 2024, Goodenough said, 'What I think happens a lot of the time is you've got climate scientists, incredible people, who are effectively doing what English people have done a lot on holiday, which is they are trying to talk to somebody who doesn't have the same language as them, and just shouting louder.'[20]

Political theorist Wendy Brown sets out beautifully what a different approach might look like, saying:

> *Only a compelling vision of a less frightening and insecure future will recruit anyone to a progressive or revolutionary alternative future – or rouse apolitical citizens for the project of making that future. This vision must be seductive and exciting, and it must be embodied in seductive and exciting leadership and movements, hopefully oriented by an ethic of responsibility.*[21]

What if. . . the rapid transition away from fossil fuels, away from industrial meat production, profligate jet-setting and economic inequality were the *making* of us? What if. . . *right now* became the most thrilling time to be alive? It is entirely possible that, in the future, we will look back on this time and think what an incredible time it was to be alive. We had the tremendous good fortune to experience it! So much changed, so fast. Wouldn't that be something?

I believe that one of the reasons – maybe even the most significant reason – we've failed so spectacularly to address the climate crisis and its many interrelated crises, sometimes termed the 'polycrisis', has to do with our relationship to the future; we must be able to envision a future we actually *want* to the extent that we muster the will to do what needs to be done in order to make that vision a reality – to the degree that it becomes our magnificent new North Star and we can't imagine doing anything else. In other words, maybe slamming the brakes on this juggernaut of self-destruction needs to be more about imagining the future we actually want and bringing that alive in people's hearts, minds and bones than it is about parts per million of carbon in the atmosphere and banners reading 'We're Fucked'?

For so many people, the future has disappeared: colonised by megalomaniacal billionaires, crushed by precariousness. It's time to 'uncancel the future', argues Luigi Vitali, editor of *Dust* magazine. 'Imagining a hopeful future isn't naïve – it's radical,' he writes. 'Without the courage to imagine a different future, we have allowed the idea of it to be quietly erased . . . Is it possible to claim a different vision for the future? When survival is at stake, it must be.'[22]

And yet, around the same time as the UN called for that 'wide-ranging, large-scale, rapid and systemic transformation' in order to avert climate disaster, the *Economist* ran a cover story with the headline, 'Say Goodbye to 1.5°C', accompanied by an image of the Earth with an arrow through its middle. The *Economist*'s cover epitomised the messaging throughout legacy media – all of it a variation on this same depressing theme: it's too late. We're screwed. The ship's going down and there's nothing we can do about it. It was fun while it lasted.

Even as I write these words in the early days of 2025, I have yet to see a single headline that reads along the lines of, 'Let's Have a Wide-Ranging, Large-Scale, Rapid and Systemic Transformation!' How would it feel to read a headline like that? Do we somehow believe we aren't worthy of such a thing? Or are we all so exhausted and run ragged in lives of increasing precarity that imagining the end of the week is already enough of a stretch, let alone a liveable future?

When did we become so fatalistic? And why is it so much easier to leap from 'this isn't a problem' to 'it's too late', than to imagine the bit in the middle where we do something useful about it? It's like waking up in the night, smelling smoke and ringing your insurance company. What happened to the part where we try to put out the fire?

Are we so overcome with dread, so paralysed by the scale of the challenge, that we can't even *imagine* putting out the fire? If so, that's ridiculous because history tells us, repeatedly, that even in the darkest hour, even when the odds look unwinnable, the tide can turn. And it can turn quickly and dramatically.[23] But only under certain conditions. And only if we can help people to fall in love with the future.

In February 1944, the French surrealist poet and member of the Resistance Robert Desnos was arrested by the Gestapo and sent to various concentration camps before finally being imprisoned at Theresienstadt. Just weeks before the camp was liberated by Allied forces in 1945, Desnos and other men were crowded into a truck and driven away. Everyone in that truck knew that they were being driven to the gas chambers. Everyone was silent, even the guards.

When the truck arrived at its destination and the back door was opened, Desnos did something unexpected. First off the truck, he stopped each person as they passed and animatedly read their palms. The philosopher and essayist Susan Griffin describes the moment: 'Oh, he says, I see you have a very long lifeline. And you are going to have three children. He is exuberant. And his excitement is contagious. First one man, then another, offers up his hand, and the prediction is for longevity, more children, abundant joy. As Desnos reads more palms, not only does the mood of the prisoners change but that of the guards too.'

The mood shifted. The guards just couldn't do it anymore. Griffin continues, 'If they told themselves these deaths were inevitable, this no longer seems unarguable.'[24] The prisoners were loaded back into the truck and taken back to the barracks.

What happened? Somehow, Desnos was able to kindle the spark of possibility, despite circumstances in which such sparks had long since been extinguished. He didn't do so by quoting facts and figures about the likelihood of their survival. No; he summoned creativity and joy and a heartfelt belief that another outcome was not only possible but achingly close. He reached through the membrane that separates the present from the future, and he dragged a future back through into the present to show people. He gave them a future to fall in love with.

Robert Desnos died, tragically, of typhoid a month after the camp was liberated, but most of those he saved that day survived the war. It was a small but heroic act of imagination, of mental time travel, from a single individual with profound consequences.

In 2023, I gave a talk in the French town of Pontivy. At the end, one of the local elected officials said that the last time he had been in this room was the previous year for a talk by Lucie Aubrac, who at the age of ninety-five was one of the few remaining survivors of the French Resistance. Following Mme Aubrac's talk, she was asked if among all the people she knew in the French Resistance, she thought they had anything in common. After a pause, she replied, 'Yes, they were all optimists.'

CHAPTER TWO

Time Is More Fluid Than We Think

It's April 2023 and Extinction Rebellion is holding a four-day event called The Big One outside the Houses of Parliament in Westminster. At its peak, around one hundred thousand people attend, demanding the UK government engage seriously on the climate and ecological emergency. I've been asked to speak, and I take it as an opportunity to try something different.

A few months earlier, I had seen a photo online from a protest during the Black Lives Matter uprising that followed the murder of George Floyd by a police officer in the US. The photo showed a young woman wearing a T-shirt with the slogan 'I've Been to the Future. We Won'.[1] It gave me goosebumps. Perhaps it's giving you goosebumps now too.

Inspired by that T-shirt, I decide that rather than talking about how dreadful things are, or about what we *could* do, or what a post-carbon world *could* be like, I would give my speech at Westminster as though, thanks to the time machine I recently built, I had just returned from 2030. The 2030 I visited was a good one – one in which we did everything we could possibly have done to avert disaster and build the future of our dreams. I want to share the thrill of what I saw and experienced there with the members of the audience. I want to make them hungry for it and to catalyse their longing. Will it work?

I change into my time traveller's costume. In reality, it's a white hazmat suit I bought from a local hardware store and a large globe-shaped spaceman's helmet that I can only wear for two minutes before the oxygen starts to run out. Sewn onto the chest of my costume is an embroidered patch. The patch is a variation of Professor Ed Hawkins's 'climate stripes', which shows a series of vertical stripes, each one representing the annual average temperature from the Industrial Revolution to the present day.[2] Shades of blue represent cooler-than-average years (mostly to the left) and shades of red represent hotter-than-average years (mostly to the right). In Dr Hawkins's original design, present day becomes increasingly dark red, a powerful and visually arresting indictment of human-caused climate change.

In my version of Dr Hawkins's climate stripes, however, the red stripes start to lighten again, moving back from lighter reds to pinks and even into light blues, the result of concerted human effort to reduce CO_2 concentrations in the atmosphere and lower global temperatures. Dressed to impress, I'm ready to go.

When my time comes, people gather around me in a circle, and I feel like a politician from the 1950s about to step up onto a soapbox. I remove my helmet, step forward and take the microphone, imagining myself part-Marco Polo, part-Phileas Fogg, preparing to share the transfixing tale of a thrilling and epic adventure.

I tell the audience that my friends and I have recently completed the construction of a time machine, and that I am going to share with them the story of a recent adventure we took to 2030. This 2030 we visited is not a utopia, and not a dystopia, but a future in which we'd done everything we could to avert disaster. I am bursting to tell them what an incredible place this 2030 is.

I describe epic bicycle rush hours, the fresh smell of the air, and medicinal and edible mushroom farms now flourishing in former underground car parks. I tell of vibrant cities, a massive reduction of cars on the roads and the explosion of rewilding efforts. I explain that people eat 80 per cent less meat but hardly anyone complains or even noticed the shift. I describe for my audience members what it sounded like – how much louder the birdsong was and how much quieter the street traffic was.

I paint pictures in their imaginations of new buildings constructed from local building materials: timber, straw, clay, stone, hemp, even mushrooms (from the former underground car parks) and how the use of cement is nearly obsolete. I report, to huge cheers, the collapse of Shell and BP in 2026, the 80 per cent decline in aviation and the closure of a second major runway in order to reforest the land. The conversation in the future is not about opening new runways; it is about the sequence in which we will close the existing ones.

'We walked down streets,' I tell them, 'filled with music, carnival, conversation, kids playing, food growing, bees buzzing. It is hard for me to express just how beautiful it was. I get emotional just thinking about it.'

At that moment, I look around the now big crowd surrounding me and listening intently, and I see tears on faces. I feel something different, in imagining the future together in this way – not only positively but also collectively. I near the end of my tale and say, 'I must go now, as I have left the time machine on double yellow lines, and you know what the traffic wardens are like in London.'

I've done similar presentations since that April day outside of Westminster, and each time I've observed similar emotional responses from audience members. Often, I bring my time machine and invite the audience to travel with me. Other times, I recount stories of my own adventures to the future.

In workshops, after we've time travelled together, I put people into groups to capture what they saw in drawings, in words and sometimes in collage using images cut from old magazines. (See 'Collage' in Travel to the Future, chapter 10, on page 147.) I've done this now with many thousands of people and the responses are pretty much universal.

Elise Boulding, who died in 2010, was a former professor emerita of sociology at Dartmouth College in Hanover, New Hampshire, former secretary general of the International Peace Research Association, and one of the creators of the field of peace and conflict studies. In 2000, Boulding published a paper in which she reflected on a workshop she'd run with a group of male prisoners at Massachusetts Correctional Institution, which strongly resonates with the time-travel exercises I do in talks and workshops. Boulding did pretty much the same exercises I do, but twenty-four years earlier. She wrote:

> *What their imaginations revealed when they mentally traveled into the future and then drew pictures of what they imagined, was deeply moving. Prison walls had melted away and all the beauties of nature and the life of free humans stood revealed: open countryside, trees, bushes, flowers, distant mountains, lakes and rivers . . .*
>
> *Everywhere in these pictures were friendly, often smiling people – walking in couples, bicycling, singing, dancing, playing games, working in small groups, fishing by a lake, growing food, offering helping hands to each other . . . Two pictured bombs dropping on a city with the caption, "THIS MUST NOT HAPPEN!" The absence of cars in these pictures was notable.*[3]

Boulding noted that these same themes of the beauty of nature and joyful community spirit had appeared in the imagined futures of her workshop participants from all sections of society for years. From members of women's and youth groups to scholars and activists, and from soldiers to diplomats, the futures they saw were bright and green, and full of happy people caring for each other.

I wonder whether, when facilitated well, this is how most people would respond to such an exercise? Boulding went on to reflect on what this experience indicated to her about the potential for actual transformation in the world, writing, 'We have many more potential co-workers in the task of building a more peaceful world than we ever knew.'[4] Might it be that there's something universal that, twenty-four years apart, both Boulding and I were tapping into here?

In another paper, Boulding argued that rather than this kind of exercise being a recent phenomenon, this tendency towards thinking positively about the future is actually what human beings have always done. And that, 'As long as we can imagine a better world with minds adequately equipped for the complexities of the 21st century, we will be able to work for it.'[5]

When I talk about time travel, I'm not talking about flights into fantasy or the absurd. That's not so useful in the context of building a positive and liveable future. Wild, imaginative and ambitious: yes. This is productive and possible within the limits of the universe. Purely magical: not so much. For example, if I fantasise about the clouds parting and dropping a huge pile of gold coins in my front garden, that's not going to get me as far as a scenario in which I perhaps buy an actual lottery ticket and then win the lottery. Mentally travelling to a future in a way that pushes the boundaries of reality as we know it, but one in which the laws of physics and biology still apply: that's what I'm after.

When I do this, something profound happens – a different kind of energy and an emotional response compared to when I give lectures about extinction and collapse (which, admittedly, I don't do too often these days). All of this leads me to wonder: what does neuroscience tell us about what happens in our brains when we time travel in this way? Why does it feel different and so much more powerful? And how we can apply that, in terms of building a future we long for?

Researchers use the term 'mental time travel' to describe our capacity to imagine the future – or the past – and how that capacity impacts our present-day experiences and decisions. While a lot of research has focused on individual future thought, more recently researchers have been expanding the focus of their attention to *collective* memory and *collective* future thought, or what they term 'collective mental time travel'.[6] This area of research recognises that as groups, whether couples planning for the future of their new family or as entire nations, mental time travel is not an activity confined to individuals. As science journalist Shayla Love, writing on the subject puts it, 'When we travel through time, we don't always go alone.'[7]

Another thing researchers have discovered is that imagining the future uses mostly the same parts of the brain – the hippocampus and the prefrontal cortex – as remembering the past. These two things – envisioning the future and remembering the past – also use the same neural pathways. Whatever goes on in our brains when we remember the past, we do pretty much the same things when we imagine the future.[8]

When we 'time travel' to the future, we dip into the cupboards of our memory, rummage around for snippets that might be useful, and then combine these snippets to create novel and unique ideas about the future. In other words, we assemble visions of the future from the resources of our past. For example, imagining what a global pandemic would be like is now far easier for most of us than it would have been a few years ago.

If I am planning a holiday to Italy and am trying to imagine what it will be like because I have never been there before, the mental picture I generate will be based on all the things in my brain that I have tagged #Italy over the years: pasta, the Leaning Tower of Pisa, coffee, mopeds and olive trees. My unconscious mind hands me a file with 'Italy' written on it. To take a different example: imagine you do nothing all day but watch right-wing news channels; it would be very difficult to imagine a fair, just and radically lower-carbon society, simply because you've not given your brain any material to work with. The cupboards are bare.

Researchers have long understood that each time we formulate a memory, our brains reconstruct those memories afresh; each instance represents a uniquely assembled combination of what's stored in our cupboards. This allows us to update our memories, making them more relevant to our current self, our current situation and our current beliefs, essentially editing our memories to make them more acceptable to who we are now.[9] Rather than being static and untainted, our memories are constantly changing, as our brains bring recollections of past experiences into line with real-time goals, self-image and self-beliefs.

A more recent revelation, however, is that something similar happens when we imagine the future: we create that thinking afresh each time.[10] According to Donna Rose Addis, a professor at the University of Toronto who specialises in perception, cognition and cognitive neuroscience, 'When you're constructing this simulation, you're essentially constructing a model of reality.' Addis added that when you imagine the future, the parts of your brain that kick in are the same parts that kick in when you read fiction or are engaged in similar imaginative activities.

I also spoke to Hal Hershfield, professor of marketing, behavioural decision making and psychology at UCLA Anderson. Dr Hershfield told me that when you time travel, part of what's happening is you're helping people paint a more vivid, more concrete, more emotional picture of the future. It's something we don't do very often and, when we do, we tend to do it superficially. 'But,' Dr Hershfield added, after I had explained my time-travel approach to helping people fall in love with the future, 'the exercise you're doing with groups is forcing people to really think about that future in a much more vivid way: give it some structure, give it some colour, give it some detail – those are the things that can then push us to want to take action.'

Addis pointed out that there is a difference between me sharing with people the vision I have of that future and them creating their own imagined vision of the future. As she puts it, 'The key is that you really need to get people to project themselves into it.' Which, in talks that are longer, and in workshops where I can create an environment in which people feel safe, is what I do. When I reflected with her on why this exercise works as powerfully as it does, Addis said, 'If you're able to get people to really think about the future in a very detailed way, where they can really place themselves in it, and it's positive, then surely you're going to be eliciting some hope. Or increasing people's hope for the future. You're increasing the plausibility of it.'

That said, it's important to acknowledge that this approach – whether I'm the time traveller describing my journey or you're the time traveller imagining and developing your own – has its limitations. It has been established that as human beings, we tend towards what scientists term 'positivity bias' when we think about the future. We recall more positive events and episodes from our past than negative ones.[11]

Also, simulations of the future are often unrepresentative, capturing the most important and noticeable elements of an experience but rarely the most likely elements.[12] Often, when people time travel with me, they describe arriving in the future on a spring day, when everything feels alive and fresh. They rarely arrive on a November afternoon when it's been lashing rain for the past five days. We often omit the possibility of personal factors that would impact our future experience (and happiness), such as a toothache, long Covid, standing in queues or the children being off school with the measles. Likewise, we tend to decontextualise broader aspects of this new scenario that would also affect that future, such as heat waves, power cuts and pandemics. We also have a tendency to overemphasise the initial part of an event – the moment we place our feet in the warm sand when we arrive on holiday, for example – but not the subsequent less exciting bits, like day four when we're sunburned, suffering from diarrhoea and have been up half the night scratching mosquito bites.

While mental simulations of the future might have their limitations, they still bring us a number of distinct benefits. Firstly, evidence suggests that positively simulating the future in our minds can be a key contributor to psychological wellbeing.[13] Secondly, this sort of mental time travel can make us more adaptable and flexible in day-to-day life. It helps us develop plans, anticipate and solve problems, and set intentions.[14] It has been shown that imagining hypothetical events makes it more likely that we will turn those hypotheticals into reality. As American psychologist Shelley E. Taylor and her colleagues describe, 'Of the many skills that humans possess, one of the most intriguing is the process by which we envision the future and then regulate our behaviour and emotions so as to bring it about.'[15]

When we invite people to fall in love with the future and to play an active role in making it a reality, the kind of future we envision – and the kind of stories we tell – matters. In 2018 while at the University of Melbourne, researcher Julian Fernando and his colleagues published a study that showed people who were asked to imagine their idea of utopia were subsequently more likely to engage in social-change behaviours.[16]

The same team went on to describe, in another paper a few years later, the significance of the *kind* of future we imagine. The researchers offered participants two different 'utopias': a 'green' utopia and a 'sci-fi' utopia. The green utopia was characterised by a drop in carbon emissions, stronger local economies and more socioeconomic equality, while the sci-fi future was rooted in technological progress and advancement. What Fernando and his colleagues found was that the *type* of utopia you ask people to imagine has a substantial impact on the degree of motivation it generates. The green utopia elicited increased motivation and behaviour change, individually and collectively, whereas the sci-fi utopia led to lower motivation and a lack of behaviour change.

Reflecting on their findings, the authors write, 'The Green utopia is likely to be seen as achievable only by active engagement in social change.'[17] In other words, it is a future that will only come about if we *make* it happen. The sci-fi future, on the other hand, feels like what we'll get if we sit back and do nothing. The creation of positive future visions inspires us to set goals (whether consciously or unconsciously) and generates anticipated positive emotion, which in turn increases the likelihood of our initiating the kind of behaviour needed to make it a reality.[18]

One of the reasons why mental simulations of the future matter so much – whether elicited by some mad English guy in a time traveller's costume or when you are yourself invited to time travel experientially as a group and to share that experience with other people – is that it becomes not only a future-visioning process but a *memory* tucked away and encoded in our long-term storage. It's what Swedish researcher David H. Ingvar called 'memories of the future'.[19] It means that the next time we try to imagine the future and we go to our memories to construct it, we find this shiny, glittery, exciting memory already there to shape our fresh imaginings.[20] Or, as Prentis Hemphill, author of *What It Takes to Heal*, puts it, 'We need visions within us that make our stomach quiver and cause us to come alive.'[21]

This reinforces what a disservice we do as climate activists when we focus exclusively on extinction and collapse. While having the tools to manage the grief and loss is vital, if that remains our sole narrative, we run the risk of reinforcing a self-fulfilling prophecy of doom and collapse.[22] Research shows that when people are experiencing an anxious or depressed mood, they are more likely to seek out stories that confirm negative views of humanity and the world. We begin to see threats and catastrophes waiting to happen everywhere we look.[23]

◆ ◆ ◆

Mental time travel is sometimes described as a one-off exercise, but in my experience, it works best as a daily practice, not unlike meditation or yoga. With a daily practice of envisioning the future, more and more details come into focus. After all, the opposite *is* also a daily practice for most of us. Every morning, we wake up and look at our phones, which fill our imaginations with messages that tell us, 'It's too late! Everyone is horrible! It's the end of the world!'

In 2013, John Whaite, a baker and winner of the 2012 *Great British Bake Off*, wrote, 'It seems that baking is emerging as a form of pill-less Prozac.'[24] Evidence suggests that the list is, in fact, a lot longer than that: growing food, spending time in nature, living on a street where solar energy is being installed at scale, being part of movements pushing for social justice, moving into a low-energy home, making and experiencing art, being part of a community organisation, riding a bicycle, writing speculative fiction, planting community food forests, learning new skills – many things that will also help us draw down carbon and move towards climate stabilisation – are all 'a form of pill-less Prozac'. All these very real activities give us the tools to help us reimagine the world while also improving our mental health. It's a matter of seeing them and using these experiences to build and populate the world we want with the sorts of experiences we value.

In August 2024, I was invited to speak on Grand Central stage at the Boomtown music festival, by far the largest audience I had ever spoken to. I had just six minutes to share some stories from the future.[25] A few days later, someone emailed me a link to a Reddit post by a young man who had been in the audience. The young man explained that he wanted to quit vaping, but he had never been able to imagine a future in which he didn't vape. He wrote:

> *I've wanted to stop vaping for about 5 years now, and yet every time I vape, it's a step towards the future where I still vape. The future where I don't vape already exists, it's not a mystical imaginary place, it's already there, it's just that I kept walking away from it. At the end of the festival I threw my vape away, didn't matter that I'd spent £50 on it, or that I knew I'd feel irritable without it. It just became completely obvious to me right then, that if I wanted to walk towards the future where I don't vape, throwing my vape away was the first step to get there. . . . That's just a tiny personal aspect of this whole thing, but the philosophy behind it can be applied to anything.*[26]

It's a small but powerful example of why mental time travel matters. It allows us to believe that other futures exist, that they're possible, that they're there in front of us, and that we can start living as though they're already here. We can rehearse different futures. It makes the necessary changes easier because we can see beyond the undesirable effort and into the desirable outcome.

CHAPTER THREE

The Superfuel That Gets Us There

I spend a lot of time speaking and teaching in the French-speaking world because, well, they invite me, and they seem to like me there. My French is lamentable (but slowly improving), so when I speak, I usually have an interpreter who stands next to me on the stage and renders into French everything I say. There is one word that often proves difficult to interpret, which is an issue, because I use it a lot. That word is 'longing'.

In many European languages, the word 'longing' is translated from English as 'desire' preceded by adjectives that increase its potency; for example, 'very, *very* strong desire'. But in English, the word longing goes beyond desire. It carries a deeper sense of yearning. It aches. It is restless. It can't sleep at night.

Longing is perhaps best described by the creator of fantastical wonderlands, Lewis Carroll, when, in *Alice's Adventures in Wonderland*, Alice finds herself too large to enter the garden:

> *Alice opened the door and found that it led into a small passage, not much larger than a rat-hole: she knelt down and looked along the passage into the loveliest garden you ever saw. How she longed to get out of that dark hall, and wander about among those beds of bright flowers and those cool fountains,*

but she could not even get her head though the doorway; 'and even if my head would go through,' thought poor Alice, 'it would be of very little use without my shoulders. Oh, how I wish I could shut up like a telescope! I think I could, if I only knew how to begin.'[1]

In over two decades as a climate activist, I've read and reread this passage many times. It speaks to one of the great frustrations I've wrestled with over the years: I believe we all want the future to be better for our children than it is for us – full of joy, health and opportunities for everyone to fulfil their own unique destiny, whatever it may be. Nobody wants an apocalypse, not really. We might enjoy them at the cinema, but we certainly wouldn't want to live through one. We want, at least, to believe that our species is capable of rising to the challenges it faces with imagination, courage and resolve. But how do we get there? Somehow, we can't seem to get our heads through the doorway.

What if our biggest barrier to that magnificent garden isn't our big heads, but the poverty of our imaginations? Or, as American writer and philosopher bell hooks once wrote, 'What we cannot imagine cannot come into being.'[2]

Most of us *can't even imagine* a future without food poverty and homelessness. A future where we embrace the challenges that the climate crisis presents with passion and enthusiasm. A future in which we wage peace with far more respect and recognition than we used to wage war. As professor of African American studies at Princeton University and author of *Imagination: A Manifesto* Ruha Benjamin puts it, 'A world without prisons? *Ridiculous*. Schools that foster the genius of every child? *Impossible*. Work that doesn't grind us to the bone? *Naïve*. A society where everyone has food, shelter, love? *In your dreams*. Exactly.'[3]

Over time, I started to suspect that, in order to hit what we're aiming for (i.e. a positive and liveable future for all), we need to cultivate *longing* for that world and the changes we need to make in order to get there, the way Alice longs for the garden. And the more I thought about this, the more I realised that real and lasting change in the world is *often* preceded by longing – a collective ache for a shared vision.

In 1865, Jules Verne published *From the Earth to the Moon*, a novel that envisioned how people might make the long and difficult journey to the Moon, weaving together the best scientific thinking of the time. Verne got a lot of things right in a way that spookily anticipated the actual Moon mission almost exactly a hundred years later.

For example, in Verne's fictional Moon mission, the number of astronauts was three, the rocket was launched from Florida, it landed safely back on Earth by splashing down into the ocean, the launch was observed by huge numbers of onlookers and the rocket was made of aluminium. As Bernd Brunner notes in his book *Moon: A Brief History*, 'Many of Verne's predictions are stunningly accurate.'[4] Other things Verne got, understandably, wrong. In the article 'Science Fiction Sent Man to the Moon', artist and author Michael Benson writes, 'Verne's lunar voyagers, depicted blasting moonward in a cannon shell fired from a giant space gun . . . would have turned into tomato juice at the moment of launch.'[5]

The book's most important, and perhaps unexpected, accomplishment, however, is that it inspired many people – scientists and children who grew up to be scientists – who were so entranced by Verne's story that they applied their lives to making it a reality. Those scientific efforts and advancements in turn inspired scores more authors, and then film makers, cartoonists, animators and others until there was so much art, film and literature that it permeated culture and collective consciousness – until success began to feel almost inevitable. *Of course* we would go to the Moon.

It didn't have to be high art, accurate or even remotely realistic to have an impact on our ability to imagine a human being setting foot on the Moon. Consider, for example, films such as 1953's *Cat-Women of the Moon,* whose poster proclaimed, 'See: the Lost City of Love-Starved Cat-Women!' The film inspired a new genre of low-budget films where male astronauts travelled to distant planets to discover all-female or almost all-female populations, including *Fire Maidens of Outer Space*, *Missile to the Moon*, *Queen of Outer Space*, *Nude on the Moon* (yes, really) and *Voyage to the Planet of Prehistoric Women.*

This interplay of science, popular culture and storytelling meant that by the time President John F. Kennedy announced the Apollo missions in 1963, it took just six years to actually get to the Moon; the average age of the team of engineers and scientists that made it happen was just twenty-eight.[6] It also meant that by the time Neil Armstrong set foot on the Moon in 1969, we'd already been there thousands of times before: in songs, in stories, in futuristic science magazines, in jazz dances, in Mighty Mouse and Popeye cartoons, in Tintin books. Indeed, Tintin cartoonist Hergé marked the Moon landings with a drawing of Neil Armstrong stepping out of the lunar module only to be greeted by Tintin, Captain Haddock, Professor Calculus and Tintin's dog, Snowy, presenting him with a bunch of flowers and saying 'Bienvenue sur la Lune, Mr. Armstrong!' ('Welcome to the Moon, Mr Armstrong!').

As Michael Benson puts it, 'Most major achievements, be they personal or collective, arrive after rehearsals. Some unfold as flights of the imagination . . . an entire branch of speculative fiction – novels, short stories and also feature films – lies behind the first human footprints on another world.'[7] In a report for UN Global Pulse, Hanna Thomas Uose notes that Franz Joseph's 1975 *Star Trek Star Fleet Technical Manual*, which purported to be blueprints from Star Trek ships in the twenty-third century accidentally beamed back to the present day, set out how their teleportation devices, ships, universal translators, medical devices and communicators worked, which in turn inspired many engineers to begin actually creating them. As Uose observes, this publication helped 'imagine devices into use'.[8]

Before *Star Trek*, there were no automatic sliding doors. The only automatic doors that existed at that time were opened by a pressure pad placed under a mat at the entrance. Even though in *Star Trek* the sliding doors were, in reality, opened by people hidden behind the scenes, they inspired the research that led to motion detectors. In the early 1980s, the first automatic sliding doors became available, created most likely by scientists who grew up watching *Star Trek*. Similarly, the iPad can be traced back to the PADD – Personal Access Display Device – that members of the crew carried around, and the 'viewscreen', which enabled on-screen discussions with other starships, no doubt sowed seeds in the childhood imaginations of the people who went on to create Skype, Zoom and other video-conferencing platforms.

In other words, the longing came first. As American author Grant Faulkner has pointed out, there is a world of difference between longing and desire. He explains, 'The kind of longing I'm thinking about is different than desire. Desire is an itch that wants to be scratched, but longing is the ache that accompanies a deep love that lives in your heart.'[9]

A desire, then, is something that can be satisfied relatively easily. We could buy that cake, take that holiday, click 'Buy' on those shoes we've found online and that desire is satisfied, that itch is scratched, although not for very long. The creation and satisfaction of our desires is at the root of the economy that we live in. It's about short cycles of dopamine, focused on manufacturing and then satisfying our desires, rather than building happiness or contentment. That is one of the reasons our economy produces so much despondency and addiction, those bleakest of states.[10]

Longing, on the other hand, dreams big, often painfully so. Prentis Hemphill, in her book *What It Takes to Heal*, describes longing as 'that vulnerable, stomach-dropping craving'.[11] As Alice discovered, getting to the object of your longing will not be easy. It exists much further out in the realms of possibility than desire does. It's possible, but getting there will take determination, some luck and intense focus. Faulkner explains, 'Desire exists in the realm of choice, but longing takes root deep in your being. It's existential. You can't just turn it off or chase it away.'[12] It's soul work.

Like travelling through space, longing for the ability to travel through time seems almost ubiquitous in Western society and storytelling, so much so that it's hard to imagine that there was a time when we *didn't* tell stories about time machines. But, in fact, before H.G. Wells wrote his novel *The Time Machine* in 1895, nobody else had written about time travel. Sure, people had written about travelling through space, about visiting the Moon, and even about falling asleep and waking up in the future; but the idea that a machine could exist that would transport you backwards and forwards to specific points in time had never occurred to anyone, at least to the point that it existed in public consciousness.

Science historian James Gleick, reflecting on this, writes, 'Somehow humanity got by for thousands of years without asking "What if I could travel into the future? What would the world be like? What if I could travel into the past and change history?" These questions didn't arise.' Shakespeare dreamed up many amazing things – magical islands, enchanted forests, ghosts and so on – but never a machine to travel through time. Nor did

Leonardo da Vinci, nor did Jules Verne. As Gleick adds, 'We have achieved a temporal sentience that our ancestors lacked. It was long in coming.'[13]

The Time Machine wasn't a hit with everyone on its publication. One reviewer wrote (with Victorian pomposity), 'We have some difficulty in discerning the exact utility of such excursions into futurity.'[14] Still, it would be fair to say that from that point onwards, the Western imagination was gripped by the idea of time travel. *The Time Machine* has been made into movies, comic books and has inspired endless other time-travel stories. Bill and Ted time travelled in a phone box in *Bill and Ted's Excellent Adventure*, Homer Simpson's toaster once accidentally turned into a time machine, and in the film *Hot Tub Time Machine*, an energy drink spilled on a hot tub's controls sends the bathers back in time. People have been gripped with the idea that time travel is possible.

But theoretically, at least, travelling through time is possible. As Gleick says, 'Time travel is easy! Einstein showed us how to do it. All we have to do is approach a black hole and accelerate to near the speed of light. Then, welcome to the future.'[15] The devil is in the details, though. The furthest we've managed to get human beings so far is the dark side of the Moon. That, and given that the nearest black hole to Earth, Gaia BH1, is 1,560 light years away, and the speed of light is 1,079,252,848.8 kilometres per hour, and the fastest a human being has ever travelled is 39,937.7 kilometres per hour, means I'm going to stick my neck out here and suggest that time travel works a lot better in theories, in daft movies about hot tubs and on pieces of paper than in reality. But if it *were* possible, how might a time machine work?

Allen Everett and Thomas Roman, in their book *Time Travel and Warp Drives*, explore in depth the kind of physics and science that a time machine would require. They set out what to them seems like the most feasible scenario for how time travel could work, before qualifying it with, 'Let us emphasise that [this] is just *pure speculation*. Presently, we have no reason to believe the above scenario is possible.'[16] Time travel exists at the very outer edges of possibility, and even then, it still looks hugely unlikely. James Gleick agrees, writing, 'We've had a century to think about it, and we will need to remind ourselves every so often that time travel is not real. It's an impossibility, just as William Gibson suspected – a magic on the order of kissing one's own elbow.'[17]

For example, on 28 June 2009, Stephen Hawking threw a party at Cambridge University as an experiment, which, he later claimed, proved that time travel was impossible. He booked a room, put up balloons, laid out some champagne and flutes as well as three trays of canapés and a giant banner that read, 'Welcome Time Travellers'. He sat there for a few hours, but not a single guest came. Then, the next day, he sent out invitations to the party, which read, 'You are cordially invited to a reception for Time Travellers', and gave the information any time traveller would need: 12.00 UT 28 June 2009, with the coordinates of the location, 52° 12' 21" N, 0° 7' 4.7" E. Shortly afterwards, he told reporters, 'I have experimental evidence that time travel is not possible.'[18]

The power of time travel, and the full potential of time machines, rests in their power as tools for storytelling. As Gleick reminds us, H.G. Wells 'didn't believe in time travel. The time machine was the handwaving—the pixie dust that helps the willing reader suspend disbelief and get through the story.'[19] I love that analogy. When I give my talks and support people in stepping out of the present and into a more fluid experience of time, when I don my space helmet and my repurposed hazmat suit, I'm sprinkling pixie dust. And the more theatrical, playful and experiential that is, the more effective the pixie dust is, the deeper it impacts people, the more successfully it enables them to build 'memories of the future' (see chapter 7, page 102).

What I've learned is that the nature of that pixie dust, and its ability to create memorable and impactful time-travel experiences, really matters. We need to find the ways to mark the transition from one time state to another. The successful sprinkling of pixie dust requires us to find the tools to mark and step across the threshold between now and where we're travelling to.

The beauty is that, thanks to Wells, time travel is something everyone understands. It's a mental shortcut, if you like, a metaphor that requires very little explanation. It allows us to mentally disengage from the present and to go on a mental adventure that wouldn't otherwise be possible. Gleick writes, 'When Wells in his lamp-lit room imagined a time machine, he also invented a new mode of thought.'[20]

When I stand up in front of a room full of people and tell them I've brought my time machine and it is going to transform the room they're in into a time machine, we are all instantly on the same page. Thanks to H.G. Wells, we are all time travellers now. We all know what to do, we all understand how it works. Everybody gets it. If we decide that our key goal in bringing about a better future is to help those around us fall in love with the future and its possibilities, then tapping into the power of time travel, building our own time machine, whatever that looks like to you, is one of the most powerful tools we have for suspending disbelief – for undermining, as American writer and activist Patrick Reinsborough puts it, 'the status quo's grand bluff: inevitability'.[21]

Charles Yu, in his novel *How to Live Safely in a Science Fictional Universe*, does a beautiful job of helping his readers consider what a world in which time was fluid and we could zip backwards and forwards at our leisure might feel like to inhabit. His character, also named Charles Yu, is a time-machine repair man who spends a lot of his time trying to find his father, lost to him in space and time. He writes of a world in which moving around in time at will is the normal state of existence for most of the characters.

'Chronological living is kind of a lie,' he writes. 'That's why I don't do it anymore. Existence doesn't have more meaning in one direction than it does in any other.' There is a passage in the book that captures beautifully how I think about time machines. In it, Charles is speaking with his father when they have a revelation:

> *He said: A house can be a time machine. A room. Our kitchen, this garage, this conversation, anything can be a time machine. Just sitting there, you are. So am I.*
>
> *Everyone has a time machine. Everyone* is *a time machine. . . . We are all perfectly engineered time machines, technologically equipped to allow the inside user, the traveller riding inside each of us, to experience time travel, and loss, and understanding. We are universal time machines manufactured to the most exacting specifications possible. Every single one of us.*[22]

Fundamentally, it doesn't matter if I believe time travel is possible or if you believe it is. What matters is that I am able to get you to suspend your disbelief and believe that time travel is possible, to break free of the shackles of linear time, even if only for a few minutes. After all, as collectors of time-travel stories Ann and Jeff VanderMeer put it, 'The truth is, fiction is one of the most effective time-travel machines in the universe and always has been.'[23]

We also need to tap into the power and potential, the radical possibility, of longing. Novelist Don DeLillo captures the importance of this beautifully: 'Longing, on a large scale, is what makes history.'[24] The key question isn't whether or not time travel is possible; rather, what would our activism look like if we acted as though it were?

PART TWO

How to Construct a Time Machine

CHAPTER FOUR

Adjust Your Disbelief Suspenders

I have the fortune – in my role as someone often invited to speak in places already doing great work to decarbonise themselves and build a new economy – to be able to see, touch, smell, taste and hear places and initiatives that most of us have been conditioned to believe are impossible. So, when people ask me for one thing they can do to bring about a more positive future, I suggest they seek out stories of real change that are happening *right now*. I'm talking about local food projects, renewable energy projects and neighbourhoods coming together to create their own solutions. This is the simplest, easiest way to start expanding your imagination – and envisioning what you want the future to look like. Once you start looking, you'll find it's happening everywhere, and that discovery will colour how you then see the possibilities in the world around you.

The fact that examples already exist in the present is evidence that the changes we are fighting for are *absolutely* possible. A 2024 study by Jason Hickel and Dylan Sullivan showed that the world could provide decent living standards for 8.5 billion people while consuming just 30 per cent of current global resource and energy use, leaving, as they put it, 'a substantial surplus for additional consumption, public luxury, scientific advancement, and other social investments'.[1] If we put our minds to it we can, as Scottish land reform campaigner Alastair McIntosh puts it, unlock 'a new constellation of possibility'.[2]

Fill the cupboards of your memory with these stories. Then, when someone says that something you aspire to is not possible, you'll know that, in fact, it is – because look over there: they're already doing it. Such stories make it easier to piece together your own vision of the future, the first steps in what Patrick Reinsborough calls 'the spark of "what if?" that grows into the conflagration of "this must be!"'[3]

Here are just a few of the many examples that I have been to see over the years – and that stock the cupboards of my own memory and my own hopes and visions for the future.

Commercial Restaurants That Cook Just with Heat from the Sun? Impossible...

In June 2024, I visited Marseille for the opening of France's first restaurant run exclusively on solar power. Le Présage, which means 'the omen' in French, is housed in a timber-frame construction with earth bricks and clay plaster made from onsite subsoil and a combination of hemp and lime infill. Two large mirrored parabolic dishes focus Marseille's abundant sunshine into the back of the restaurant's ovens. Hold a piece of wood in the place where the heat reaches the back of the oven, and it immediately bursts into flames.

I first visited Le Présage back in 2021, when it was little more than a kitchen in a shipping container – albeit a solar-powered kitchen in a shipping container, even then – in the middle of an overgrown plot on the edge of Marseille. On that day, I met founder Pierre-André Aubert, who had big plans. He had recently been granted planning approval and funding to build France's most ecological restaurant. His plan was for a timber-framed, highly sustainable restaurant, surrounded by food gardens, a food forest and ponds, with food waste-generated biogas for those rare days when the sun doesn't shine in Marseille. An on-site wastewater treatment system would be capable of cycling clean water to irrigate the gardens.

When I first visited in 2021, I asked Pierre-André to describe Le Présage in 2030, after it had been built and had had a few years to get established. He gathered his thoughts.

'Welcome,' he said. 'It's been almost seven years now since we opened the big restaurant. And we still exist, which means people came and enjoyed our food.'

Warming to his storytelling, Pierre-André gestured to the scrubby field surrounding us. 'You see the gardens: it's quite amazing. We said to everyone it's going to take at least five years until we really use the garden because, you know, trees have to grow! We have fruits from our trees and it's so beautiful, I can't tell you. The whole garden is quite amazing because it's working with the restaurant. We set the restaurant up as a single organism. It's not just a garden with a restaurant, it's really an organism and it works well. It's just so . . . lush.'

Pierre-André described how in this 2030 the model they pioneered had spread to other places around Marseille, and that the planting of edible forests has seized the public's imagination. He reflected on what it had felt like, back in 2021, to be a pioneer of such an unusual idea. 'We showed that, actually, crazy ideas are only crazy for the ones who believe they are crazy,' he told me. 'Back then, we were saying that we need some imagination, that we need to tell stories about another future. That's what we did. And today we are telling people we can do things differently; we can step away from the normal traditional paths and, sometimes, well, it works – and it's beautiful.'

I was transported. I could see this empty plot through a new lens, as though its future was being projected on top of reality. Not only could I see it, I could smell it, feel it, taste it. I could even hear the trickling water in the ponds, the bees sucking on the flowers, the voices of the gardeners chatting and laughing as they harvested the day's produce. I felt, as Pierre-André described his vision of 2030, that I was standing not in the 2021 prototype version of Le Présage, with its shipping container and polytunnel, but as though I had fallen through a time slip to 2030.

And then, fast forward only three years, and there I was again, being served food in the newly completed Le Présage at its formal opening. On a scorching hot day, the place was packed with local residents, friends of the project, local and national politicians, food writers and others. It was so wonderful to see this dream realised, and to taste the delicious food emerging from the kitchen of Pierre-André's imagination, some of it flavoured with herbs already growing in the garden. It's like tasting the future.

Later, over email, he explained the meaning behind Le Présage's name to me. 'Presage' is an anagram of the French word for asparagus, *asperge*. He explained that as a child, he would go foraging in the hills around Marseille for wild asparagus in the spring and became quite good at finding it. 'To me,' he said, 'it's the perfect example of the true luxury we need to come back to.' He explained his understanding of luxury: something offered by nature for a short time, some knowledge, and some time to take advantage of the opportunity – and, of course, the taste.

'Le Présage is cool because it means, at least to me, a good omen for a delicious future!' he said. Indeed, the backs of the staff's T-shirts are emblazoned with #FuturDélicieux, which means 'delicious future'.

A Truly Local Food System? Impossible. . .

The town of Mouans-Sartoux in the southeast of France is home to 10,500 people and a remarkable revolution in food production. In the local schools, 100 per cent of the food served is organic and 80 per cent is grown in a 6-hectare municipally-owned local market garden.[4] Students help out in the garden and the harvest is freshly prepared in the school canteen. The local authority budgets this at the same cost as the national average; this is possible because food waste is 75 per cent below the national average, which saves 20 per cent, and 50 per cent of the meals are vegetarian, saving an additional 20 per cent, according to Deputy Mayor Gilles Pérole.

The positive impacts of the project extend beyond the school, rippling out into the community. Since this initiative began, 59 per cent of people in Mouans-Sartoux have changed their diets, decreasing the amount of ultra-processed food they eat by 30 per cent and the amount of meat they eat by 23 per cent. On a daily basis, 28 per cent of residents eat organic produce, as opposed to France's national average of 15 per cent.[5]

I've been to Mouans-Sartoux. I've stood in the market garden and seen the food growing. I've visited the city's food-skills training centre, La Maison d'Éducation à l'Alimentation Durable (Centre for Sustainable Food Education) where kids learn to cook; it's not a state-of-the-art kitchen, just a simple kitchen with a domestic cooker because that's what most of the students have at home. I've visited the school and seen the fresh produce being prepared on site. I've sat in the canteen while the kids eat lunch. I can tell you without hesitation that, compared to most other schools I've visited, it feels amazing to eat lunch prepared in such a system.

While it is true that in the present day we have a food system that channels money to shareholders, drives down the quality of what we're feeding our children and drains money out of local economies, don't let anyone tell you that something different is 'impossible'. I've seen it. And it works. Why settle for less?

Car-Free Urban Districts? Impossible. . .

One of the most ambitious car-free neighbourhoods in Europe is the Vauban district of Freiburg, Germany. The site of a former French barracks, Vauban is now home to 3,000 people, covering

41 hectares of land. In 1993, the citizens of Vauban decided they wanted a different kind of development and campaigned for three years to make it happen. They established a process that incorporated their current social and ecological concerns, as well as ideas and dreams for the future. The final scheme prioritised the development of housing cooperatives and individual and community-based builders over private commercial developers and investors.

Vauban shows what's possible when ecological design is put front and centre. Most new houses are built to high energy-efficiency standards, many to Passivhaus level, and there are solar panels everywhere.[6] Vauban residents get their energy from a combined heat and power scheme augmented with solar power generated on many of the buildings' rooftops.

Apartment blocks are built in different styles and colours, most with balconies covered in plants. Inner courtyards are filled with trees where tiny birds dash between the branches. Throughout the neighbourhood, mature tree stands have been preserved and many more trees have been planted, so large parts of Vauban feel like forest. Apple trees, plum trees, pear trees and walnut trees abound, and grape vines scale the buildings. The barracks themselves have been turned into student accommodation, a community centre, nurseries, a primary school, cafes and restaurants, shops and other social enterprises. An expansive park is managed as a nature area.

All of this is remarkable, but there's something else that is even more inspiring. Vauban was redesigned in such a way that residents do not need to own private cars. The neighbourhood is serviced by trams that travel into the city centre approximately every five minutes. Car-free bicycle and pedestrian routes, lined by mature trees and a swale to return runoff to the water table, intersect the centre of Vauban. Kids as young as three pedal around on little bikes, as cargo bikes carrying two or three children lumber along nearby. Bike storage facilities are everywhere.

There are many footpaths closed off to cars entirely. On the streets where cars are permitted at all, residents are allowed to drive their cars (in the unlikely event that they own one) to the door of their homes for drop-offs but must then park in the community car park, a multistorey structure with solar panels on its roof. There are just 172 cars for every 1,000 residents, far fewer than Germany's national average of 585 cars per 1,000 people.[7] The nearby city of Stuttgart, for example, has 531 cars for every 1,000 residents.[8]

Something you might notice most if you visit Vauban, however, is not only how different it looks from most modern European neighbourhoods, but how different it sounds. Without the constant background hum of the internal combustion engine, you begin to hear things in more detail, a greater granularity. As I walked down one street, I listened to someone taking a piano lesson in their home; I even could hear people's knives and forks on their plates as they ate lunch.

There are many planners, architects and investors who would tell you that a creating a place like Vauban is impossible, ridiculous even. But I've been there, and I can tell you: they are wrong.

Cities Redesigned to Make Cycling the Dominant Mode of Transport? Impossible. . .

In 2022, I visited the city of Utrecht in the Netherlands, home to 370,000 people, which I had heard was home to 420 kilometres of bike paths and 21 bicycle parking facilities, accommodating a combined total of 30,000 bikes. The largest of these facilities – and the largest such bike park in the world – has space for 12,500 bicycles. Every day, 33,000 cyclists use Utrecht's busiest cycle route. To visit the city centre, 56 per cent of the city's residents use bicycles and 94 per cent own at least one bicycle.[9] Only 15 per cent of trips into the city centre are by car.[10]

It wasn't always this way. There was a time when Utrecht was like most other cities, and the Netherlands was as much a motoring nation as other European countries. But then, in the 1970s, a number of high-profile accidents in which children were killed by cars, as well as the growing awareness of the risks of dependence on imported fuels for cars prompted by the oil crisis of 1973 and 1979, inspired active citizens groups to push for transportation changes in the Netherlands' cities.[11] In 1971, it was especially bad on the Netherlands' roads: 3,300 people were killed by cars that year, more than 400 of them children.[12]

When the Dutch journalist Vic Langenhoff – one of whose children was killed in a traffic accident and another injured only months later – wrote an article called '*Pressiegroep Stop de Kindermoord*' ('Pressure Group Stop the Child Murder'), the slogan 'Stop the Child Murder' spread like wildfire across the country. Activists blocked streets to create play spaces for children, occupied spaces where cyclists and pedestrians had been hit by cars, and went out under the cover of night to paint illegal bike lanes.[13] A 1972 film tells the story of how children in the neighbourhood of De Pijp mobilised to close streets to cars and create 'play streets'. One of the children who was interviewed for the film remarks, 'That's how you campaign. Show what is wrong and how it could be better. Then the city will follow.'[14]

These efforts emerged from and dovetailed with the counterculture of the 1960s, which nurtured a coalition of groups who visibly campaigned for greater self-governance; smaller and more liveable neighbourhoods that encouraged walking and cycling over cars; and opposed economic growth for its own sake.[15] By the 1980s, the building of a new cycling infrastructure was well underway across the country.

Today, visit the Netherlands and you'll discover 35,000 kilometres of cycle paths and a country where over 25 per cent of all trips are by bike. (In the UK, that figure is a pitiful 2 per cent.[16]) The Dutch government invests €0.5 billion per year in road and parking infrastructure for cycling, which is also an investment in public health, preventing approximately 6,500 deaths per year and contributing an additional six months in life expectancy over the European average.[17] These improvements in public health also save an estimated €19 billion a year.[18]

Building this kind of infrastructure is not an expense; it's an investment, and it's taking off in the UK too. Research has found that the public health benefits of investing in Low Traffic Neighbourhoods in outer London can be up to a hundred times greater than the cost, with those benefits increasing over time.[19]

Other cities are also moving forward ambitiously. Ten years ago, if I saw a cyclist in Paris, I wanted to take them home for a cup of tea and check they were OK. Now, thanks to the city's mayor, Anne Hidalgo, there are more and more bikes there each time I visit; 2023 was the first year on record that more people travelled by bicycle than car – 11.2 per cent versus 4.3 per cent – in Paris's city centre. As recently as 2010, cycling accounted for just 3 per cent. The city is investing €250 million over six years to build an ambitious safe infrastructure, with the aim of the city being 100 per cent cyclable by 2026, having already built over 1,000 kilometres of new cycle paths.[20] It's like seeing a city come back to life.

Getting Rid of Concrete from Urban Spaces? Impossible. . .

In March 2024, I was invited to give a talk in Val-de-Reuil in Normandy, a town built in the 1970s – the golden age of concrete. It was a beautiful evening, so before the event, Anne Lehelloco, the town's head of sustainable development, energy performance and mobility, took a group of us for a stroll. We visited Dominos, a local school that had been 80 per cent depaved in response to rising temperatures that made the schoolyard too hot for pupils to use during warmer months. Anne showed us a photo of what Dominos looked like in 2023 prior to depaving; it was a flat expanse of cracked concrete and tarmac.

Since then, however, most of the hard surfaces have been peeled away, planted with twenty-six young trees and relandscaped into terraces to absorb rainwater. The result is that the kids now use much more of the space, and the teachers report a huge improvement in the acoustics, the space now being far quieter. According to Lehelloco, the municipality now has an annual depaving budget of €300,000, and €100,000 a year for establishing more tree canopy.[21]

Depaving is on the rise throughout France and around the world. The city of Leuven in Belgium is one of the world's most climate-conscious cities and the only city in Belgium where cycling is now the preferred mode of transportation, with public transport second and the private car third. Leuven's municipality has a team dedicated to depaving the city and a budget of several million euros a year for the task. It even has a 'tile taxi' – a truck that will remove and reuse depaving waste free of charge.[22]

In the Netherlands, depaving is practically a national sport. Started in 2020, NK Tegelwippen is a national championship that challenges cities and towns on who can remove the most paving slabs. At the end of each year, the municipality that has removed the most tiles wins the coveted 'Golden Shovel' or 'Golden Tile' awards. A panel gives out a 'Tile-Tipper of the Month' prize.[23] At the time of writing, the removal of tiles has led to 863,636 square metres of newly depaved areas becoming available for landscaping and other uses. Of the 342 municipalities in the Netherlands, almost 200 now take part in the challenge. Football clubs have become involved, too. At some grounds, supporters can hand in depaved tiles in exchange for a small piece of turf from their team's pitch. The NK Tegelwippen website keeps track of the running total of removed tiles, both for each municipality as well as a national tally, which currently stands at an impressive 14,475,439.[24]

How far could a depaving revolution take us? A 2022 study explored the potential of depaving in Melbourne, Australia, and identified 6.6 to 24.5 hectares of hard-surface parking, which translates to about 11,000 parking spaces, that could be depaved while still providing the city with sufficient parking.[25] The potential benefits included between 31 and 59 hectares of new tree canopy, cooler urban spaces and biodiversity 'stepping stones' that would link habitats across the city. The study also cited mental health benefits, including a reduction in loneliness and potentially dementia. It would improve air quality, reduce flooding and offer economic benefits. 'This single land use reallocation tactic could deliver substantial, integrated ecosystem service improvements in highly urbanised areas,' the authors wrote.[26] Perhaps by 2030, the depaving industry will be the single biggest source of new employment where you live?

Time Travel as a Tool for Revitalising an Economically Depressed Industrial Town? Oh, Come On...

The town of Dudley in the West Midlands is probably not the first place that would come to mind as a time-travel destination. Home to about eighty thousand people, Dudley has suffered high unemployment and poverty following the closure of the steel industry. But in late 2020, an organisation called CoLab Dudley put out a call for residents to come together and explore issues of intergenerational justice, long-term thinking and rebuilding imaginative capacity in planning the city's future.[27]

CoLab's Lorna Prescott, one of those responsible for the invitation, wrote at the time, 'Our Mission: to travel to 2031 with local people and return with Memories of the Future.' The group has organised various events and projects, including workshops to reimagine Dudley High Street; the development of a one-hundred-year Cultural Strategy; and the Dudley People's School for Climate Justice, which aims to increase climate resilience for both the local residents and the local ecosystem. The Dudley CoLab also cultivates a network of 'Time Rebels' to catalyse imagination, cultural projects and creative experiments related to the city's future.

Why did they choose the name Time Rebels? Lorna and her colleague Jo Orchard-Webb explained to me that 'time' is a powerful way of challenging business as usual, that different futures are possible, that we have things to learn from the past, that we have agency in the design of the future, and that it is a gentle way of introducing ideas around intergenerational justice. The term 'rebel' offers the promise of changing things deeply and radically in a way that doesn't add to the existing sense of precariousness. They suggested that even a wider movement of Time Rebels would still need to be place-bound, working closely with all aspects of life in a particular place.

Beavers as Better Hydrological Engineers than People with Degrees in Hydrological Engineering? Impossible. . .

One summer evening in July 2022, I visited Woodland Valley Farm, a three-generation 69-hectare organic dairy farm in the gorgeous rolling Cornish countryside near Ladock run by Chris and Janet Jones and their daughter Felicity. I travelled there with my wife, Emma, because I had heard that the Joneses had reintroduced beavers in 2017 and that it had dramatically changed the landscape, for the better. We wanted to see it with our own eyes and learn what they had done, and why and how it had impacted the land.

We arrived just as the afternoon was turning to dusk, the best time to see beavers, and Chris took Emma and me on a tour of this remarkable landscape, as he regularly does with groups of schoolchildren and various organisations. Stepping into the fenced-in 2-hectare beaver enclosure required to get a licence for reintroducing beavers felt a bit like visiting a very benign version of Jurassic Park – it looked like landscapes I know, and yet it felt deeply different: more alive somehow, home to a large mammal, native to the UK, a keystone species but one I had never seen before.

The first things I noticed were the many small streams, the sound of running water and the birdsong. Then, I began seeing the small trees felled by the beavers and their tell-tale teeth marks on the stumps. Since the beavers have been at Woodland Valley Farm, they have engineered six new ponds, eight 'leaky dams' built from mud and sticks, three new streams and increased surface water storage by 1,790 cubic metres. Their work has been nothing short of miraculous.

Benedict MacDonald, author of *Cornerstones: Wild Forces That Can Change Our World*, argues that beavers manage wetland better than conservationists. 'They conspire with time to create the most diverse of landscapes and to slow the powerful flow of fast-running rivers in more innovative ways than the most skilled of human engineers.'

As Emma, Chris and I approached the main pond, surrounded by trees and so peaceful, we noticed the 'plip plop' of fish jumping in and out of the water. The average size of the fish in the ponds has doubled since the beavers arrived, and insect and bird populations have exploded. Ten new species of birds have been recorded there, three new mammals and eleven species of foraging bats.[28] Research at other beaver reintroduction sites shows that the way beavers alter the landscape creates new habitats for invertebrates and amphibians too.[29] The place is teeming with life, and you can feel it.

Chris tells us that these ponds hold a lot of water, reducing the risk of flooding in nearby Ladock, which has previously experienced serious floods. Research has shown that during times of heavy rainfall, these beaver ponds reduce peak flows of water by as much as 60 per cent.[30] The ponds also trap silt and nutrients that would otherwise eventually wash out to sea or cause eutrophication downstream. The 'leaky' dams constructed by the beavers from mud and sticks hold back water, but they also create more streams, moderating rather than blocking the flow. As MacDonald continues, 'So complex is the world created by beavers that scientists are still unravelling it.'[31] The ponds also act as water storage for the rest of the farm. During the 2022 droughts, aerial photos showed other beaver sites from the air. They were oases of green among dry, yellow grassland. These remarkable creatures have also built more reservoirs in the three years between 2021 and 2024 than privatised water companies combined have built since 1989.[32]

The moment we first saw a beaver swimming across Chris and Janet's ponds will always stay with me. We couldn't stop grinning. It was magical. As Chris told us, 'The best thing about having beavers on your land is the look on people's faces when they first see one. It's just a gift.' It was love at first sight. I was smitten.

There are now an estimated 1,000 reintroduced beavers in Scotland and 500 in England.[33] In Europe, the population is estimated to be around 1.5 million, which represents quite a comeback. At the start of the twentieth century, beavers had been hunted to almost to extinction for their prized scent glands, their meat and their remarkable fur; only 1,200 remained in all of Europe.[34]

In North America, the population has rebounded from a low of 100,000 to approximately 15 million.[35] Ben Goldfarb, the author of *Eager*, told me, 'There are explorer's accounts of crossing the state of Indiana and not finding a dry place to camp for 100 miles because beavers had so thoroughly impounded water all over the Midwest. Today, that same area is strip malls and cornfields essentially. When we lose beavers, we lose the ability to imagine what a natural, diverse, complex, biodiversity-filled landscape looks like.'[36] In the US, beavers are celebrated as 'nature's firefighters' for their role in preventing forests near their ponds from drying out.[37]

It is estimated that in one year, the landscapes created by beavers in the northern hemisphere sequester greenhouse gas emissions that would cost $75 million to capture and store by other means – an extraordinary service we get for free.[38] Given that carbon capture and storage (CCS) technology is very expensive and yet hugely underdelivers on what it promises (leading one climate policy commentator to remark, 'Carbon capture isn't a technology that likes to be built'[39]), then it becomes crystal clear that we need an awful lot more beavers.

Beavers do their vital work for free, unlike privatised water companies, which have withdrawn £85.2 billion in dividends from England's ten water and sewage firms since they were privatised in 1989.[40] All the beavers ask is a few trees to chew. Most beaver introductions take place on private land and through wildlife organisations. As report after report comes back pointing out the incredible impacts beavers can have, more and more landowners are welcoming them back, sometimes through the 'official channels', and sometimes not (a process known as 'beaver bombing').[41]

For many decades now, the modus operandi among many farmers has been to get rid of as much water from the land as possible to maximise arable land. To some farmers, living alongside creatures whose natural tendency is to bring that water back can be a challenge, but it's not insurmountable given the potential enormous benefits. As Chris told us that July evening, 'If you have a stream or a river without beavers it's like a little garden bonfire of biodiversity. If you put beavers in, it's like throwing petrol onto the bonfire. There's nothing else like it in the temperate world for bringing life.'

If you want evidence that change can happen and happen quickly, look no further than this humble ecosystem engineer, this realiser-of-the-impossible.

◆ ◆ ◆

I've given you a few examples of people who have been willing to suspend disbelief long enough to see the impossible take place before their very eyes, but I could just as enthusiastically have described any of the following:

- The construction of Le Haut-Bois, a nine-storey apartment block in Grenoble, France, built with local timber, sequestering rather than releasing carbon, as concrete does.[42]
- A non-profit in Liége, Belgium, called the Ceinture Aliment-Terre Liégeoise (Liége Food Belt) that is reimagining the local food system, including an initiative where the city makes undeveloped land available at low cost for new food-production enterprises.[43]
- A French construction company whose employees grow and distribute vegetables each week for every one of the company's seventy employees.[44]
- The French mayor who initiated the development of straw-bale cooperative housing, a 1.2-hectare market garden that produces 250 baskets of food a week for local families and numerous renewable energy projects.[45]
- And many more. . .

All of the above makes the world a better place, and all would make the world an even better place if scaled up hugely.

The world is full of examples of things that we are told are impossible but that actually exist and function perfectly well. Once we start looking, we find that so much of what we are told is impossible is nothing of the sort. That 'wide-ranging, large-scale, rapid and systemic transformation'? It already exists somewhere. Go and see it, and then adapt it to where you are.

CHAPTER FIVE

Learn from the Pioneers

Creating memorable opportunities for people to step into the future, or into the past, is a largely untapped approach in activism, certainly in climate activism. But if you know where to look, there are inspiring practices and activists from both within and beyond the climate movement from whom we can learn a lot. Roman Krznaric, social historian and author of *History for Tomorrow* described these people to me as 'time rebels':

> *I think of the Time Rebels as a huge movement that already exists, but may not yet have been named. There are people explicitly working on futures, whole industries of people engaged in futurology or people in the design world, at Stanford where they all work on futures. There are the gardeners, who think about futures when they're planting stuff. There's every immigrant in a boat with their children crossing the Mediterranean thinking about their children's future. There are artists . . . doing work around time. There are writers like you or me who are trying to change the ideas in the world around time. They're already here, a lot of them, this Time Rebel movement. A lot of social change is about telling people they're part of something bigger.*[1]

His explanation – that they're already here – stayed with me. I began to realise I already know people like this, working away in their own communities, creating time portals, creating imaginariums, creating immersive tastes of the future, reaching through time and pulling the future into the present. Pioneers all, for sure, and often brilliant eccentrics, but they each hold vital pieces of this puzzle, and each, in their own way, point us towards what a larger movement framed around positive futurism might look like.

The Amateur Ancestor Tours

You know those endless rooms in museums full of stuffed animals and birds with glassy eyes, those permanent collections of pinned butterflies and models of bewildered-looking sea creatures, those dusty steam engines? The museums you visited on school trips and then never again? If you take one of Justine Boussard's Amateur Ancestor tours, the first of which took people around the collections of the Science Museum, the Natural History Museum, and the Victoria and Albert Museum in London, you will find yourself interacting with those collections through new eyes, experiencing time in a wholly different way.

Those stuffed birds with the small placards of information? Justine uses them to open a conversation: 'How did we end up relating to nature in this way?' For example, Justine uses 'Hope', the huge skeleton of a blue whale that hangs in the Hintze Hall of the Natural History Museum to initiate a conversation about the whaling industry. She then uses storytelling to project participants forward seven generations into the future to explore what our relationship to whales could be like at that time, as well as an exploration of the kind of world such a relationship would foster.

Justine's tours are designed to give people a time-travel experience that takes them into 'deep time' and enables them to make new connections between, for example, natural history, industrial heritage and contemporary design. 'We literally travel through time,' she tells me. 'You don't see the world the same afterwards.' Some participants leave with a feeling that deep time is no longer an intellectual concept but rather something they have experienced, and an understanding of it that then permeates their life and work. Others see and experience complexity in a way they never have before.

I was curious as to what Justine has learned when leading these tours – about how best to enable people to become time travellers, how to encourage them to trust you and follow your lead in becoming more playful in their understanding of time. What makes a good enabler of time travel? 'I think you need to believe in it yourself,' she told me. 'If you come to someone and tell them, "You know what, suspend disbelief for a minute and just come with me, and let's see where that takes us," if you yourself believe in it, they're more likely to come.'

I love this idea that our time machine can actually be what's around us – museum collections, landscapes, architecture, people – which we can skilfully use as storytelling prompts that turn participants into time travellers. In the early 2000s, I worked as a permaculture teacher in Ireland and would do an exercise with my students called Permaculture Tour Guides. I asked them to imagine that it was ten years in the future, and that the ideas from this course had, in the years following it, spread into this place and deeply transformed it, to the extent that now visitors come from across the world to marvel at this permaculture paradise. Their job in this future is to act as the tour guides, taking groups round to local housing estates to marvel at this incredible place.

I would ask one group to design a ten-minute tour visiting the food-production elements of the place, another group to describe the water-conservation elements, another the energy elements and so on. The tours that resulted were animated, compelling and such fun. I always wondered what the residents of the very ordinary housing estate made of this group of people having their attention drawn, with huge passion, enthusiasm, and a lot of pointing and gesticulating, to their lawn and car-parking spot. Once we embrace the need to create opportunities for people to see the present through different lenses, to overlay what could be onto what is, the creative opportunities are endless.

You Are Not Here

Mushon Zer-Aviv is an artist, designer, writer, technologist and an Israeli peace activist based in Tel Aviv who uses a similar approach that he calls 'speculative tourism' as a way to help people use imagination to draw deeper connections. In 2006, Mushon created the 'You Are Not Here' walking tour of Baghdad via the streets of New York. Mushon and his collaborators produced a printable map of New York that when held up to the light allowed participants to see through to the streets of Baghdad. As people reached New York landmarks that aligned with certain Baghdad locations, they would discover a sticker with a phone number allowing them to access an audio story about that location in Baghdad.[2] Mushon describes his work as operating 'at the crossroads of science fiction, historical tourism, Augmented Reality and local action'.[3]

In 2007, Mushon collaborated with Palestinian blogger Laila El-Haddad to create a map that overlaid Tel Aviv and Gaza, allowing people in Tel Aviv to experience, through Laila's stories, what it would be like to walk the streets of Gaza. As Mushon describes it, 'The city came alive, not only as a set of stories, but also as a physical experience in my body. The way Laila loves her city is revealed to me in the way I love my city.'[4]

More recently, Mushon brought together eight artists, activists, journalists and authors to write stories based on different walks around Jerusalem, guided through the user's smartphone, as part of the 2017 Jerusalem Design Week. For him, the idea of helping people experience different futures in Jerusalem was a jarring one. 'The future of Jerusalem is a hyper object of pain,' he told me. 'Jerusalem is terrified of its future. The visions for the future are very violent, very exclusionary, to the level that nobody touches the future of Jerusalem.'

The project's ultimate goal was to overlay eight different stories, offering the opportunity for, as Mushon puts it, eavesdropping on the future. Each story sat somewhere between the polarities of utopia and dystopia. In one, participants visited archaeological sites of the City of David in the East Jerusalem neighbourhood of Silwan, a contentious site whose history right-wing Jews summon to claim exclusive land rights over the entire city. In the story that unfolded, narrated by the founding members of the Palestinian–Israeli movement A Land for All, participants found themselves immersed in a future in which the city and its history was now shared, with the growth of mutual culture and traditions across Jerusalem. The project's unique approach, Mushon argues, offers the opportunity for 'more complexity, more contradiction, forces going in different directions and evoking a more nuanced reading of the future.'

'There was something so beautiful about jumping into the future to look differently at the past,' Mushon told me. He admits to having been sceptical about A Land for All's ideas prior to the project, dubious that its aims could ever be realised, but the experience moved something in him, he says, and he is now an active member of the organisation, and a part of its leadership.

Mushon and his colleague Shalev Moran explain on their website that the goal of speculative tourism is 'freeing the political imagination, while shedding light on local identities and reacquainting ourselves with our lived environments; we use fiction and speculation to reveal different ways of taking responsibility for our habitats and our future'.[5]

I asked Mushon how this future-orientated work has altered his perspective on activism.

> *For a long time, when it comes to activism around the conflict, I felt like the work I've been doing has been stuck in symbolic representations of injustice. I felt guilty about speaking about injustice without understanding how does it stop? There is something about human rights organisations (in a lot of cases) and even in environmental organisations, many of them strive to document the present, and they have no clue, and sometimes no interest, in imagining anything different.*
>
> *They say 'the truth will set you free', but too often, the truth will not set you free. The truth would make you complicit, the truth would make you numb, the truth would depress you, the truth would corrupt you. We are overwhelmed by the present and by our inability to imagine anything but the present. Dystopias say, "Everything we love and know is in the present, and what the future can do to us is to take it all away from us." I say no. We cannot cling to the present . . . We have to think more widely about futures.*[6]

Town Anywhere

Experiences that allow people to step across into the future and experience it in an embodied way, and to rehearse how they might act in such a future, can be deeply impactful. Town Anywhere (originally called Transition Town Anywhere), is a process developed by community arts practitioners Ruth Ben-Tovim and Lucy Neal in which a large group of people, in a large space, mentally time travel to the near future, imagine their role in that future, seek out others who share a similar vision, and then build that future world using cardboard boxes, bamboo canes, sticky tape and string. They inhabit this world, trade in it, celebrate in it.

When I spoke to Ruth, she told me that although she had facilitated the exercise many times now, she had never actually taken part in it herself as a participant. For a recent event in Hull, East Yorkshire, she had a group of apprentices facilitating different parts of it, which freed her up to be able to take part for the first time.[7] 'There was a *relief* in being in the future . . . A real sense of freedom . . . There was a release valve about being able to be in the future that took me away from the kind of anxiety, the fear, the struggle that we can feel here,' she explained. 'When I was in the future and we were making and creating, there was a sense of possibility that you don't often feel in the present. . . When I came back into the present, it actually made me feel a kind of lightness of starting things,' she described.

In August 2024, Ruth and I ran Town Anywhere as part of the Forwards Festival in Bristol, South West England.[8] Ninety people spent the day travelling to 2035 together. During the lunch break, we asked everyone not to dash straight to their smartphones, which would suck them back to 2024, but to spend lunchtime still in 2035. Rather than overhearing conversations that began with, 'So, what do you do?', we overheard conversations that began with, 'So, what work were you doing back in 2024?' And, perhaps more importantly, 'What do you do now?'

I often hear the words that Ruth used to describe her experience – 'when I was in the future' – from others who attend my workshops or talks, and it reassures me that this experience of creating memories of the future is vital. To step into an imagined future in a way that generates positive emotions, in a way that feels embodied, and in a way that is memorable enables our brains to store that experience as a memory for the next time we set out to think positively about the future.

The Atmos Project

In my own work, I try to create 'utopian moments' that invite the past or the future into the present, to give people that experience of 'when I was in the future'. One of my favourite examples took place in my hometown of Totnes, Devon. It's July 2021, that point in the Covid pandemic where public gatherings are permissible, but only if people wear masks and stay one metre apart from each other.

Everything is set up and ready to go. In the back of a white transit van are two powerful projectors worth £125,000 on loan to us free of charge, accompanied by our projectionist Tim Dollimore who is making final adjustments on his laptop. Everything has been tested, and everything works. A generator purrs on the pavement next to the van. I'm nervous. Will anyone turn up? Or will too many people turn up?

We are outside the gates of a derelict former Dairy Crest milk factory in Totnes, where I live. A group of volunteers who will be stewards for the evening arrive in their hi-vis jackets, and as it begins to grow dark, the public – three hundred people, all told – start to arrive. Once the audience is assembled, we begin to project visuals onto the derelict site's chimney and onto the roof of what is known locally as the 'Brunel building', named after Isambard Kingdom Brunel, the Victorian-era engineer who designed it.

We start with a short video that tells the story of how the site was sold two years earlier on the day before the community was to sign a contract to become its developer, in what would have been the most ambitious community-led development project – aka the Atmos Project – ever in the UK.[9] The crowd learns how the community still had a £2.75 million grant from the National Lottery Heritage Fund being held for us to renovate the building onto which the film was being projected in order to turn it into the best music and arts venue in the southwest of England. 'We are determined to get the site back,' one of the speakers in the video says. Then artist, music producer and composer Brian Eno appears on screen to introduce what was to follow.

'The Atmos Project represents a sort of beacon for the future, a vision of how things could and should be,' he said. 'At this critical time in history, we need more than anything else probably, ways in which people can come together to cooperate creatively and we certainly need it more than we need another development driven solely by developers' self-interest.'[10]

Then *77 Million Paintings,* Eno's light painting, which creates abstract artworks that slowly change and are always new and previously unseen, flickers into life, accompanied by a beautiful sparse piece of piano music Eno composed just for the evening. Just as Sydney Opera House had been a few years before, the roof of the Brunel building and the site's chimney are transformed into imperceptibly changing mosaics of colour. It's haunting, dazzling and deeply affecting. It's like being in an outdoor cathedral. The final voice in the video that has introduced Eno's work says, 'Enjoy the show. And just think, we could be doing this every night.' It evokes a future in which the Brunel building is now the southwest's leading music, art and theatre venue, a place where spectacular and extraordinary things now happen on a regular basis.

This gorgeous and deeply touching event summoned that future into the present, turning 3.2 hectares of derelict and abandoned buildings, which one of my co-directors of the project, Frances Northrop, describes as 'a rotten tooth' into something magical, enchanted, beautiful. It prefigured the site's future, the future that the huge majority of the town had dreamed together, voted for, campaigned for, and connected us all to it. Ever since the community had embarked on their campaign to bring the site into community ownership back in 2007, our intention has been to help people to fall in love with the future of this site. By bringing together music, art and community and creating an emotional, powerful sense of living as if this change has already happened, we enabled people to step into the future, even if just for an hour.

New Constellations

New Constellations is a small UK organisation run by Iris Andrews and Gemma Mortensen that invites participants to envision more hopeful and intentional futures – by 'mapping new constellations of hope and possibility'. They ask participants to imagine that they can connect with the place they live; then to ask questions, such as: what do I love about it? What can I learn from its past? What needs to be left in its past, and what might be the stars that guide its path into the future? We are all guided by constellations of stars, it's just that currently, humanity is collectively being guided by the wrong stars: stars that are guiding us towards great peril.

In late 2020, New Constellations ran a campaign with radio ads and a billboard in Barrow-in-Furness in the northwest of England stating that, 'The future belongs to those who believe in the beauty of their dreams.' Posters invited people to call a freephone number and answer the question, 'What's your boldest dream for Barrow?' and also to nominate people they felt should be members of the crew.

Fifteen people representing a diverse cross section of the community were chosen. Funded by a £50,000 grant from the

National Lottery Emerging Futures Fund, each of the 'travellers' received a box in the post containing candles, chocolates and numbered envelopes that contained prompts such as 'What is Barrow to you?', 'Where is the light?', 'Where is the dark?' and 'What does the outside world say or think about Barrow? How does that make you feel?' They were asked to visit places in or around the town that meant something to them and to call a phone number and leave their reflections. The group then met several times a day over Zoom and engaged in discussions, meditations, origami making, journaling and storytelling, set within the framework of the phases of a journey they were about to embark on together:

1. **The Shore.** Any sailor about to set out on a voyage into the unknown starts by standing on the shore reflecting on the place they are about to leave. What they love about it, what needs to change, its light, its darkness, exploring their guilt, nostalgia, pride and love, and any anger and regret they might associate with the place.
2. **The Rigging.** They need to check their masts, sails and general seaworthiness, throwing off any beliefs that might inhibit confidence and openness to possibilities.
3. **Departure, At Sea and Fertile Void.** Sailors will feel a mix of excitement and trepidation, voicing questions such as 'What am I doing?' and 'Is this even necessary?' Once departed, they may initially feel 'all at sea', but they learn to surrender to the ocean's currents until new constellations begin to appear and their vision adjusts.
4. **Crow's Nest, Astronomy and Orienting.** This is a time of quiet contemplation up in the crow's nest, identifying new constellations of stars to guide them, coming back down and sharing their initial insights with their fellow

travellers and reflecting on how they might guide them moving forward.

5. **Wayfinding.** They begin their return journey back to land, feeling the sense of camaraderie and courage from fellow travellers. They return to where they started, but seeing it, and its possibilities, with fresh eyes.

The resulting constellation took the form of a beautiful poster, based on a star map, which captured the main insights and observations from the process. It acts as a distillation of the new 'stars' formulated by the group, a reminder of a new direction.

New Constellations also produced a set of twelve cards, each one representing one of the new 'stars'. These cards pose questions for reflection each time a decision needs to be made about the future. For example, the 'Leave no one behind' card asked, 'Will this benefit all of Barrow, leaving no one behind? Who do we need to understand and take with us? Are we working street to street to share the opportunities we are creating?' The 'Invest in us' card asks, 'Does this support communities in Barrow and give opportunities to young people, local businesses, makers and innovators? Are we backing and supporting local people to create a good local economy and good work?'

The Constellation was formally adopted by the local council and is now being used to inform decisions across the borough, including plans for new community hubs, new approaches to community policing and a new Independent Advisory Group featuring some of those who went on the journey. One participant, describing the vision of Barrow they were left with by the process, described it as 'a big star providing a guide point for other towns and cities across the world'. It connected people to the past in a way that helped them to see the possibilities of the future through new eyes.

Inheritance Day

Celebrated every year on 12 December since its inception in 2015, Inheritance Day imagines a world 150 years in the future where people have worked out 'how to live in harmony with each other and the planet'.[11] The Terran Collective, the California-based group who founded the event, say of this time:

> *War is a thing of the past. The global community has committed to ensuring that every person has food, shelter, and healthcare, and poverty has been for all intents and purposes eliminated as all our energies are focused on thriving and abundance for all. We have learned how to live lightly and sustainably on the planet, there is plentiful renewable energy for all, and the climate has been restored to a healthy balance. Women, LGBTQIA, and people of all cultures, colours, and religious beliefs have equal rights worldwide.*[12]

The date was chosen to mark the adoption of the Paris Agreement in 2015, which the group explain was the catalyst for everything that led to this future. To find out more, I spoke to one of Inheritance Day's founders, Tibet Sprague. He told me that the event was initially conceived as a gathering somewhere between Passover and Thanksgiving, to look back over the arc of history and to honour the huge sacrifices previous generations made to create their present-day world. It is centred around a ceremonial dinner, which is prepared collaboratively through cooking together or by guests contributing to different parts of the meal.

The first celebration was such a powerful experience that the group realised it should be an annual holiday, celebrated by everyone. Tibet describes taking part in Inheritance Day as 'a really profound, fun and powerful way to tap into inspiration and hope, and get reactivated and committed to doing our part to create a better world.'[13] Every year, Tibet and his friends invite different people to join them, bring in different facilitators and experiment with new elements. The ceremony is always led by a woman or a genderfluid or non-binary person to symbolise a world that has moved beyond the patriarchy.

The dinner follows a ritual that consists of five courses, which are called 'bells' because a bell is sounded to mark the transition from one part of the ritual to the next. Each bell marks a key tenet that this future was built on, which are expressed by different dishes that add to the story being told:

Bell One: A Culture of Care. The first part of the ceremony honours matrilineal connections and the balance between masculine and feminine that came to define this future. The dishes shared represent life and the feminine, such as eggs and seeds.

Bell Two: Justice, Healing and Reparations. Ancestral traumas, such as racism and oppression, and the losses and grief they caused are recognised. Bitter foods, such as cacao pods and uncured olives are eaten in acknowledgement of this. However, this is then followed by something sweet, such as chocolate, to represent human kindess and liberation.

Bell Three: Equity and Abundance. The third course celebrates living in a world where everyone's needs are met with a universal basic income and universal healthcare, and there are no more billionaires. People get up and dance and then eat dishes that contain all the food groups – as Tibet puts it, 'platters of abundance' – which are representative of a world where no one goes without.

Bell Four: Harmonious Ecology. The world's ecosystems have been brought back into balance, which resulted in a resurgence of biodiversity. In this round, people eat balls of black rice to represent coal and black hummus to represent crude oil as a way to symbolise the recarbonising of the planet.

Bell Five: Global Peace and Unity. People are invited to name and celebrate the highlights and turning points from the last 150 years, such as the ending of all wars and the removal of political borders. A stew is shared that contains all the colours of the rainbow to symbolise the peaceful and inclusive world people now live in.

I asked Tibet why he has taken part in Inheritance Day every year. 'Honestly, I get chills every time I talk about it. The feedback I get from people who take part is: "We rarely get the time to imagine a better future; we worry about the future but spend our time in the present. To step into and imagine the best possible future we could bring forth and to embody it, feels really good." It really does inspire people to think, "Well, what if that is possible? What do we need to do to get there? How can I do something different in my life to participate and contribute to moving us towards that?" It sparks a sense of possibility in folks that doesn't always exist and that can then lead to shifts in their lives and different actions. I feel this in myself every time I do it.'

◆ ◆ ◆

There are so many different ways to travel through time; the ones I've mentioned here are just a tiny selection. What they have in common is their ability to give people an embodied experience after which they can say 'when I was in the future', and they each work in a way that is not focused on how to design better products or be more profitable. They are all committed to helping people ask the bigger, deeper questions, to fundamentally reimagine the world they see around them.

None require huge budgets or yet-to-be-invented apps or new technologies. They are about making different uses of things we already have around us, seeing those things through new eyes, using storytelling and imagination to help people see them in different ways. They all embrace the sensual, trying to make this reimagined world as real as possible, a complete experience. They are all playful, and they all harness the power of storytelling but with a straight face. They all take people on a journey, starting with the premise that the future isn't fixed, that we can still mould it into something else.

I'd like to introduce you to three individuals who have been experimenting with what it means to be a time traveller in your own community.

Annaïg Plassard is from the small town of Plabennec in the far northwest corner of France, in Brittany, population about nine thousand people. One day in November 2023, dressed in a silver space suit and helmet, Plassard walked through the streets of Plabennec handing out invitations. Later that day, she rode through town on horseback, in the same attire, holding a placard reading '*Je reviens du futur et nous avons gagné*', which translates to 'I've been to the future. We won'. Plassard rode her horse into the petrol station and dismounted on the forecourt to feed it hay where others would more usually park to fill their cars with petrol.

It is affecting, heroic almost, to watch Plassard passing through her community in this way, like a modern-day Joan of Arc – bold and affirming and slightly ridiculous. A few months later, she attended a huge demonstration in Nantes against the resurgent far right's victory in the first round of parliamentary elections, dressed in her silver time traveller's suit and space helmet, and carrying her sign. Interviewed later by *Ouest France*, after her photo went viral, Plassard said, 'A lot of people came to see me. There were smiles and thanks. This sign is like a flag that gives hope.'[14]

Plassard produced a film for French TV called *Retour à Plabennec* (*Return to Plabennec*), which broadcast in September 2024, to document her journey of starting a Transition group in her town and how she embraced the role of a time traveller to mobilise her community. A few months after the programme was broadcast, I caught up with her to find out what the response had been. She told me that she received lots of positive feedback, including from people who were inspired to start a Transition group in their own community and inviting her to speak at a screening of the film in their own community.

In Plabennec, Annaïg has now formed a Transition core group, and is supporting other communities inspired by the film who want to do that same thing. 'I see our local initiative as a facilitator and incubator for small and big citizen projects,' she told me. She said that personally, she feels she is shifting, professionally, from being an artist to what she calls a 'transition activator'.

Educator, writer, public scholar and spoken-word artist Walidah Imarisha has also shared her work with me. Walidah co-initiated a project with writer adrienne maree brown called *The People's Encyclopedia 2070*, an act of what she termed 'collective liberatory dreaming' and a demonstration of time-travel-based storytelling. The original idea was to create entries for an encyclopaedia written in 2070, in a future where, as she puts it, 'we have been winning every battle'. The team described their workshop thus:

> *It has been 50 years since the historic Civil Rights/Liberation Movements of the 1960s and 1970s. In this workshop with Walidah Imarisha, participants will imagine themselves 55 years in the future, and engage in writing entries for the 2070 People's Encyclopedia about current issues/events now, as a way of imagining how the world today can lead to the*

world we want. At the end, each participant will have a zine made during the workshop to take with them.[15]

'You are either talking about real existing issues or movements or people, or you are making up future incidents or movements,' Walidah told me. People might write 'this is when the last prison closed', and then set out some key events along the way that made it happen. She gave an example: '"In 2030, folks rose up and had sit-ins and die-ins and pushed for this legislation, and then in 2050 because of this . . . coalition. . ." Right? It allows that change, that first seems so unrealistic, to actually seem like a few concrete steps away to think about. And with the kind of timeline of saying, OK, well in five years that actually does seem like maybe that is realistic. And then in ten years after that, that does seem realistic. And then we're there.'

For Walidah, the power is in writing these momentous social transitions as facts. As she told me, 'An encyclopaedia entry is, "This happened. This was the year that we abolished prisons. This was the year that borders were eliminated." It is a fact. It is a futuristic certainty in the same way that there are historical certainties. I believe that that helps us claim these futures with the same strength and tenacity that we claim the past. Those futures exist. We just have to make them. But they are a certainty. They are not a possibility.'

The workshop was first run in Detroit in 2015 at the Allied Media Conference. Walidah worked with organiser Morrigan Phillips to design the workshop, partly as a response to the 2014 Black Lives Matter protests. Walidah told me, 'Creating tangible temporal items like the zines allowed people to feel like they were physically touching and engaging with the future they had collectively dreamed up.' She has run this workshop over twenty times, with youth groups in prisons, on university campuses, in community centres. Most people write entries in an encyclopaedia format, some people just draw. The experience, though, of time travelling to a future that turned out the best it could, is often a deep and touching one for those taking part.

Lastly, Andy Clee is a former Royal Engineer and member of Plastic Free North Devon who created a time machine for Earth Day in Braunton in April 2024. Clee's device combined an entrance chamber and transition space made from offcuts of wood and recycled tent material, which led into a comfortable dome tent. Outside, a large sign read 'Departures' and a poster listed 'Prohibited Items' (despair, cynicism, fear, anger, negativity, doubt, pessimism, selfishness), and a 'Travel List' (optimism, imagination, creativity, joy, fun, fearlessness, hope, togetherness) as well as an invitation to 'wait here for the next take-off slot'.

Once enough time travellers gathered, Clee told them, 'I'm newly qualified. It's the first time I've done it and I'm allowed to take people on my provisional licence ten years into the future and we're only going six, so we should get back OK.'

Next to the entrance to the inner space, Andy had made a red handle that could be pulled down from 'Open' to 'Lock' ('I always wanted to build one of those,' Andy said). Once inside, he asked his travellers to lie down, close their eyes, travel in their imaginations to the future, and then come back and draw what they saw. 'Maybe it allows people to relax,' he told me, 'and if you're more relaxed then maybe you can become a bit more creative.' After we'd finished our conversation, he sent me an email with a key thought that had slipped his mind when we spoke: 'I forgot to mention that we discovered that cake is a very effective cure for anyone suffering from a bit of "time-travel sickness".'

Annaïg, Walidah, Andy. Eccentrics or pioneers of a positive futurism movement of time travellers? You decide. I'd say both.

◆ ◆ ◆

Perhaps by now, like me, you are also starting to imagine a movement that sets out what it's for as much as what it's against. That recognises these times as the *beginning* of something thrilling rather than as the *end* of everything. A movement where you can't tell the difference between activists, artists and social entrepreneurs. A movement that turns future dreams and visions into real action in real places in the real world, rooted in the telling of stories about the future that those projects will lead to.

This would be a movement that uses all the different creative tools at our disposal to tell tales of a future so irresistible that it galvanises a new North Star for people to follow. A movement that recognises that the best practitioners of the radical imagination and of time travel are often marginalised and oppressed people from across the world, and the need to amplify their insights and act as good allies. It would be a movement that forcefully and clearly dismisses the myth that change is always slow and rarely occurs.

I feel like we are in a time where, while there are many amazing things happening, far too many people, organisations and governments are all sitting and looking at each other, using each other's inaction to justify and embolden their own inaction. It's a kind of mutually reinforcing downward spiral, one that hails 'pragmatism' as some kind of virtue rather than the shameful walking away from responsibility that it actually represents. In reality, what we need is to be able to see that the inspiration our boldness, our courage, our audacity, can inspire in others is what unlocks similar courageous acts and, in turn, trust that that will lead to the creation of longing at scale.

CHAPTER SIX

Organisations as Time Machines

Helping people to fall in love with the future needs to come from everywhere: from business, national government, regional and local government, from community organisations, education establishments – everywhere. What I've found fascinating during the research of this book is examples of local governments and other organisations who are beginning to develop new relationships with time, in particular recognising that their work needs to support the people they serve to fall in love with the future, as well as supporting them to make it a reality.

Local governments are, in some ways, in a stronger position to do this than many other organisations, and in other ways in a weaker position. They usually have more access to resources than community organisations, and they have the potential to build new structures and new policies that could be transformative. As we will see, they can create 'enabling infrastructures' that can unlock new practices.

But at the same time, local governments often move more slowly than community organisations can, weighed down by bureaucracy. Some of the examples in previous chapters, though, show the degree to which deeply imaginative and creative local governments can transform things. What would a local government, or any organisation responsible for enabling change, look like if it viewed its task as enabling people to fall in love with the future, to become the facilitators of time-travel processes and deep imagination?

Bannau Brycheiniog National Park

The Bannau Brycheiniog National Park (BBNP) in Wales is one of the UK's fifteen national parks (it was formerly known as the Brecon Beacons National Park). It covers 135,000 hectares of some of the most spectacular landscapes in the country, whose sweeping grandeur is attested to by the millions of people who visit it every year. It is home to 33,000 people, their work, customs and foods, as well as to gorges and waterfalls, caves and sink holes, limestone pavements, open uplands, small woodlands, rivers, lakes, farmed landscapes, hedgerows, country lanes, stone walls and the many elements that make up the landscape.

The BBNP is also home to rare whitebeam trees and uncommon Arctic alpine plants, such as purple saxifrage. It is one of the last outposts for Welsh mountain ponies and hosts rare upland birds, such as red grouse and golden plovers, as well as rare lichens and mosses. It is one of my favourite places. Time slows down when you're there, and on a clear day the views are so spectacular they fill you up with space and peace and beauty. It's also a place where the impacts of climate change are already being felt. As the BBNP states, 'Already in the National Park we are experiencing the impacts of a destabilised climate – from extreme heat, drought and water scarcity, to extreme rainfall and flooding. This is affecting people's wellbeing and livelihoods – from farming to public services and businesses – as well as impacting nature.'[1]

In 2023, the BBNP produced its management plan for the next ten years. Such plans tend to be quite dry, but here was something different: a visually arresting and inspiring document with colour photographs, poetry and postcards from the future, alongside artists' impressions of how the landscape in the park might change over time.[2] It was a magical creation that transported readers into a future that 'could be' and was simply 'not yet'.

This management plan arose because previous plans hadn't succeeded. Stakeholders felt that this time around, they needed a plan that shook people awake to the challenges facing the BBNP and also inspired them with visions of what the park could be – one that spoke to the heart, not just to the head. This approach was made possible, in part, by the 2015 passage of the Well-being of Future Generations Act, which compels policymakers to consider how a policy will impact – and, ideally, improve – the wellbeing of future generations.[3]

The Well-being of Future Generations Act has already led to changes. In 2019, First Minister Mark Drakeford cited it in his decision to cancel the £1.6 billion M4 motorway relief road around Newport. This, in turn, led to the cancellation, two years later, of *all* new road-building schemes and a proposal to plant 86 million trees in nine years.[4]

Helen Lucocq, the strategy and policy manager of BBNP, explained that the law 'gives us the permission to act. Without it, we couldn't have written this plan.' Helen's colleague Liz Hutchins, senior policy advisor at BBNP, added, 'You have to keep repeating it and to embed these practices. You have to keep making that future liveable and believable and keep building on it.'

The BBNP team members told me that in their work to embed the management plan in the park's community, they have now begun to use time travel as a tool, and plan to do more of it. When I first spoke to Helen, she told me, 'We want to create a time-travel extravaganza, to use the past, present and future to help people navigate. We want to create honeypot events, where people are excited to know that time travel is coming to their town, that they want to be there and to be part of it. We need to create a space that is experiential that you can get large numbers of people through.' A time portal, in other words. It was the first time I had heard someone from an organisation of this size talking in this way.

A few months later, I heard from Helen that their first pilot time-portal experience had taken place. Liz and Helen joined forces with local creatives Eleanor Greenwood, Jodie Bond and Chris Briton. They took a mobile planetarium owned by BBNP and transformed it into a time machine. The first part of the project involved working with young people in local schools. The team made two short videos, one in black and white, showing the food system of the late 1940s and how the National Park fed itself at that time, and another showing the challenges of the food system today. Both were presented to students from a local school by 'time-travel facilitator' Eleanor, projected onto the curved walls of the planetarium / time machine. The young audience was then invited to make their own short videos, working with supportive creative people to help them.

The intention is to follow this up with events where the young people invite local decision makers to join them in the time machine, this time sharing the videos of the past, present and future, and to begin exploring how to actually get there, how to make these futures a reality. When I caught up with Helen, the first of these sessions between young people and decision makers had just taken place. She said she was overwhelmed with the support the project had garnered in such a short space of time, and how just after this one run through, her email inbox was already filling up with requests for repeat sessions, and ideas from other groups and councils about how the time machine could be landed as part of wider policy discussions.

The experience from this pilot, she told me, is that a time-travel-based approach can be a powerful way of sidestepping the 'consultation fatigue' that can be observed in many communities, and that these playful, creative approaches can build a kind of futures literacy in participants vital to unlocking fresh thinking about the future.

'As policymakers we always seem to start the wrong way round,' she went on. 'The adults get together and think about how they can better bring future-generation thinking into decision making. The refreshing thing about this approach is it starts with the perceptions of young people, and young people hold the space in which decision makers are then asked to think - it totally shifts the dynamic – it's so powerful. All the adults that participated in the workshop kept talking about how impressive the young people were in their thinking. They seemed surprised – I think it was because no one has ever really given the kids the voice. It's always been there, we just weren't listening.'

The BBNP team members are also reflecting on how this process might lead to a place where people don't just say, 'I've said what I want, now you need to do it', but instead creates an infrastructure that empowers people to step in, self-organise and make things happen. 'How do we flip the paradigm,' Liz asked me, 'so it's the public sector enabling and catalysing and signposting people to what they can take part in now?'

Connecting the Culm (CtC)

In 2022, I was asked to consult on a project called Connecting the Culm (CtC), led by the Blackdown Hills Area of Outstanding National Beauty (AONB) in the southwest of England, to help protect and enhance the River Culm and its catchment in the Devon countryside. CtC brought me in as a 'time-travel consultant', a first for me, to help create a long-term plan for the river that would have the maximum level of local support and establish actionable steps for addressing floods, drought, water quality and ecosystem health for wildlife and people.

I wanted to help the project's stakeholders imagine, through the use of my time machine, what that future might look like. We ran three workshops over Zoom, in which we travelled to the year 2050 to witness a flourishing river catchment now resistant to flooding and drought, sparkling in the spring sunshine, teeming with fish, and supporting flourishing communities alongside and around it.

I've conducted similar workshops before, but this time we added one magic ingredient I hadn't used before: an artist named Richard Carman who lives and works in the Culm catchment. After the group travelled to 2050, I asked them to form into pairs and reflect on what they saw, smelled, felt, heard and tasted and to then feed that back to the larger group. As the participants did this, Richard started drawing.

As the participants shared their visions about the future they saw, Richard drew fast, impressionistic sketches to capture what people were saying. They described better access for walkers, better paths and gateways, communities more involved in looking after the riverbanks, cycle paths along the river, more orchards and nut trees, small-scale food production, lower densities of cattle, re-established hedgerows, expanded wetlands, the return of salmon and trout up the river, more water vole sightings, outdoor classrooms connected to local schools and beavers transforming landscapes.

Richard then came back onscreen and shared his sketches, asking, 'You mean like this? Is there anything that needs changing or adding?'

Those rapidly drawn images were a dynamic way to capture the process and to invite people to add or make suggestions to what Richard had already captured on paper. I then asked the participants to think about some questions they might ask in the present day that would unlock that 2050 future. Their suggestions included:

- What if pesticides, herbicides and artificial fertilisers were banned?
- What if decision makers listened to the ideas of children and young people?
- What if all farming was driven by environmental needs rather than annual crop income?
- What if we could stop soil loss?
- What if Fore Street became Fore*st* Street?
- What if beavers were everywhere?
- What if mowing lawns was a thing of the past?
- What if the water in the Culm became drinkable?

Several months later, I was invited to be a speaker at the launch of their Blueprint for the River Culm, a long-term management and investment plan for the river. Proposals in it included the establishment of new floodplain meadows, building 'scrapes' and swales to allow the return of water to the water table, new woodland plantings including orchards and agroforestry, upgrades to water-treatment works and measures to keep pollution out of rivers. Before the presentations began, I took time to browse the displays and was thrilled to see detailed final drawings Richard had created based on those initial sketches. It felt like the art, dreaming and longing had gone first, and now here were the practical steps for realising them.

Moral Imaginations in Camden

It's November 2022, and I'm in a meeting room several floors up in the building that houses Camden Council, the local authority for the London borough of Camden. The views from the large windows across the city are impressive for a country boy like me. I'm there to observe and then participate in the world's first 'Imagination Activist' training delivered to the staff of a local authority. It feels momentous. It's the first time I've heard of deep imagination and time travel being taught in such a setting.

The training is the work of biologist and systems thinker Phoebe Tickell, founder of Moral Imaginations, a pioneering organisation dedicated to tackling the climate crisis through collective imagination and kinship 'with the human and more-than-human worlds, present, past and future'.[5] Launched with support from then council leader and now Labour MP Georgia Gould, the training forms part of a larger project to build what Phoebe calls Imagination Activism, which is 'a new kind of activism that focuses on what is possible and what we can imagine, rather than fighting existing systems'. Crucially, the shifts in imagination allow organisations to build their muscles of imagination, which lead to structural changes that meet and support the imagination of the community.[6]

In the session I'm sitting in on, the final day of the training, participants in small groups are presenting their final projects. They've been asked to describe different aspects of how the council operates in the 2030 of their dreams. The first group begins its presentation, talking from the perspective of today, and what they imagine would be happening in 2030.

Phoebe gently interrupts and says, 'Try it again. Imagine we are already in the future. It's 2030 *now*. Tell us about what has happened as if it's real.' The energy in the room shifts.

We then hear thrilling stories of what this transformation looks and feels like, presentations that start with 'here in 2030'. As Phoebe later recalls, 'It put a smile on people's faces. It plays with your brain, . . . It gets around the cynicism and the rational brain, which is saying "this isn't real, this hasn't happened". Suddenly, it feels very real. It makes it more believable. It's like a magic trick.'

For Phoebe, embedding imagination and time-travel skills into an organisation requires three key elements:

1. **Time and Space.** Shifting worldviews and changing thinking takes time, and sowing seeds and changing culture and behaviour requires the organisation to consciously dedicate time and space to it. Building imagination capacity requires removing the obstacles that are getting in the way of it.
2. **Permission.** Getting those working within an organisation to feel sufficiently emboldened to ask big questions, deeply reimagine the world and that organisation's role in it, and to travel to different future versions of it requires that the organisation first gives them permission to do so, and to create a culture in which it's OK to appear silly or make mistakes.
3. **Practice.** The organisation needs tools it can use to embed these practices into the daily culture of the organisation. In Camden, for example, tools include starting meetings with a five-minute exercise imagining the future so that the meeting can proceed with an expanded sense of possibility, as well as asking: 'What if every major strategic meeting includes the voice of the future generations?' Camden even created a community of practice, composed of people who completed the training and then continued to meet and to support one another, along with a budget to further embed these practices.

For Phoebe, one of the key aspects of time travel as a tool is its playfulness. 'I'm a scientist,' she told me, 'which really helps, because science tells us about the limits of our knowledge and gives us licence to challenge the established consensus. Quantum physics is showing us all sorts of limits to our understanding of time and space, so who can say what is possible? The science fiction author Arthur C. Clarke said, "Any sufficiently advanced technology is indistinguishable from magic." So, let's question the ways things work and fall in love with that sense of possibility.'

Imagination Activism has since been rolled out to other local authorities and groups in Sweden, Norway and Denmark, as well as to organisations such as the London Marathon and IKEA. I see so much potential in this, especially at a moment when many organisations, be they municipalities, national governments, businesses, NGOs – whoever – are all looking at each other and waiting for someone else to jump first. Training like this opens a vital space within each organisation to expand a sense of what's possible, encourage greater ambition and build a core of people prepared to reimagine everything.

I ask Phoebe why it's so important to empower individuals and organisations to fall in love with the future. She tells me, 'We absolutely have to. The only other option is to fall into despair and apathy. It's not about a thin, shallow hope, it's not about optimism, it's not about thinking it's even the most likely thing, but it's about, in the worst possible odds, choosing a love of humanity, of the planet, and of the future existing. Choosing love over despair and apathy, choosing to believe in the common good and the best of human beings in a time with so many dreadful things happening.'

Building 'Enabling Infrastructure'

If local authorities and institutions like BBNP are serious about supporting their communities to time travel, to imagine and express the futures they long for, then how best to support them in making their imaginings a reality? The worst thing would be to open up these possibilities but then for people's experience to be that nothing happens, and all that care and enthusiasm just dissipates.

I would argue that local authorities, and indeed any organisation that supports people in making changes to their worlds, need to create 'enabling infrastructures' that make turning dreams into reality possible, which smooth the way for community groups to step up as effectively as possible and make ambitious things happen. 'You want to start a community farm? A community-led housing project? A community energy company? Then here are some tools, policies, support and funds that will greatly assist you in making your visions of the future a reality. Go for it!'

A good example of building an enabling infrastructure comes from Denmark. Astrid Hørby Aller is a member of Borgerrepræsentationen, Copenhagen's City Council, and deputy mayor for technical and environmental affairs. In 2022, Hørby Aller was contacted by two community groups wanting to improve their streets but lacking the funding to do so. Rather than just giving out piecemeal funding for different projects, Hørby Aller decided to create a programme of funding within the City Council that such projects could apply for. In 2023, having secured some money to enable a request for proposals, she was blown away to receive eighty-one applications! This first round of funding focused on creating car-free spaces, on depaving and on ambitious reimagining of spaces. In that first round, €1.5 million was distributed to three streets.

The following year, a second round of funding enabled a new request for proposals. This time, projects were invited that focused less on the creation of car-free areas and more on redesigning of streets and parking areas to free up space for people, nature, play and trees. The costs of removing hard surfaces and preparing areas for tree plantings had proved very high in the first round, so the next ambition was to achieve more for less. In the second round, €1.8 million was shared among community groups on six streets. The third round, planned for 2025, will allocate €2.7 million among ten projects. In the 2025 scheme, streets will be allowed to remove as well as reorganise parking spaces, with plantings in large containers rather than removing the existing surfaces.

I was fascinated as to why Astrid felt there was so much interest in the first round when the request for proposals was first announced. She told me that Copenhagen is a creative place, with many residents who see the city as 'malleable', a long history of citizen action, what she calls 'a tradition of meddling' and a culture of not waiting for permission. The creativity and ambition was there; the blockages were about whether people felt allowed to act, and where the funds might come from. And so she made the process as simple as possible; applications were kept to a single page. As Astrid told me, 'It has become a central project of mine to make the city more like play dough.'

I could also have pointed you to municipalities who have created policies and support structures that make it easier for community organisations to create urban agriculture projects, community renewable energy initiatives, urban biodiversity initiatives or community-led development projects. The point is, if organisations are going to invite those that they serve to time travel, to expand their imaginative sense of what's possible, they then, I would argue, need to meet them halfway, making it so much easier to turn their imagination into reality.

◆ ◆ ◆

The concept of creating well-facilitated spaces within large organisations for the reimagining of those organisations and for skills around time travel is starting to gain traction in different settings. UN Global Pulse is an organisation that acts as the UN Secretary General's Innovation Lab. They describe their work as being 'at the intersection of innovation and the human sciences to inform, inspire and strengthen the ability of the United Nations family and those it serves to anticipate, respond and adapt to the challenges of today and tomorrow'.[7]

In November 2024, UN Global Pulse announced, in partnership with UN Innovation Network and Beyond Lab, the formation of the 'Department of the Possible', a series of workshops for UN staff and others designed to bring imagination, creativity and long-term thinking into the process of transforming the UN, and also how people work across the UN to achieve its goals.

In 2023, UN Global Pulse had published a report called *The Most Creative Look to the Future: Imagination and Creative Practice in Service of Organizational Transformation*, which set out the case for placing imagination at the heart of the UN's practice. The Secretary General has spoken about the need for a UN 2.0, and the report recognises that reimagining at such a scale is a muscle that needs to be built within the UN.

The report argues that art, imagination and creative practice will be vital to this transformation. It makes five recommendations for 'starting points' from which this work could begin. The first is Emergent Strategy, inspired by the work of adrienne maree brown, which suggests not planning too much, but instead inviting artists into a process that is open to seeing where it wants to go. The second is Embed Artists, which advocates for making space for artists within teams or organisations, not as artists-in-residence, but as equal members in discussions and planning. They write, 'Just by placing them in decision-making spaces, where they are rarely allowed, disrupts the status quo and allows rules to be broken and norms to be challenged.'[8]

The third recommendation is Multidisciplinary Residency, which calls for bringing in people from a range of disciplines and skillsets: designers, chefs, economists, poets, policymakers, etc., coming together for periods of intensive work, in ways that they design together. The fourth is that, in the same way that the report recommends embedding artists, they also Embed Youth, intentionally inviting young people to be part of these processes. The final recommendation is Prefigurative Practice. In the spirit of rehearsing the worlds that we want, this is about creating opportunities for rehearsing the future, telling stories of the future together, dreaming together, creating shared 'memories of the future'. The report notes that within UN Global Pulse's Finland team, they use this principle to 'practice the worlds we want' and 'rehearse the future with our team'.

For anyone seeking to build, within an existing system, a time portal, the capacity to harness time travel to increase possibility and to accomplish far more ambitious goals, these five principles are an excellent place to start. I asked Lauren Parater, creative strategy lead at United Nations Global Pulse, who had commissioned *The Most Creative Look to the Future,* for any additional advice for anyone inside a similarly large institution wanting to build capacity for imagination and temporal fluidity. 'Find examples of other organisations who are doing this already,' she told me. 'And find your allies, both within and outside your organisation. Leadership cares what others say about your work!'

Lauren introduced new practices into her team. For example, when planning new projects the team now starts with a visioning exercise imagining what this project could have achieved ten years into the future, what ripples and knock-on impacts it could have generated. Now, when such projects are presented to the wider organisation, the presentation begins with this vision, an approach Lauren has already seen move other staff members to tears. 'This stuff moves people,' she told me. 'There had been such resistance to this work and this was the first moment I felt openness to it.'[9]

CHAPTER SEVEN

Make It Immersive

We saw in chapter 2 how important it is, in terms of helping people to fall in love with the future, that we find skilful ways to enable them to create 'memories of the future'. I want to share here some tools I have found to be powerful ways of doing this. In my own talks and workshops, I use visualisation, storytelling, audio recordings and other activities as tools that help people break free of their moorings in the present and step into the future in a multisensory way.

For example, Field Recordings from the Future is a project I have been creating in tandem with this book, a collaboration with ambient music artist Mr Kit (whom you met in the Introduction).[1] I visit places that already sound like the future needs to sound like (car-free neighbourhoods, urban mushroom farms, landscapes being rewilded by beavers and so on) and make recordings, which Mr Kit then weaves into immersive pieces of ambient electronic music, designed to cultivate a 'nostalgia for the future'. We are also creating immersive experiences with audio and video projections of places and projects we've visited that people can experience by lying back in a deckchair and stepping into the future.

I've loved the process of gathering these field recordings. There is something powerful about really tuning into the sounds of a place, but at the same time imagining that what

I'm listening to is actually the sound of the future. I remember one morning in Utrecht, in the Netherlands, sitting in a tunnel near the train station through which runs one of the most-used cycle paths in the city. I had imagined when I went there that I knew what a city's bicycle rush hour would sound like: the passing of wheels, the ringing of bells. But as I sat there, on a cool and grey Utrecht autumn morning, and tuned in to what I was listening to, I began to hear greater and greater nuance and granularity.

These passing cyclists were not just a lumpen mass of vehicles making the same noises, like a car rush hour might be. Rather, there were people taking three or four kids to school in one cargo bike, the kids in exuberant conversations with each other. There were people cycling while chatting away on their phones, saying good morning to their friends and families, and those so into their music that they were singing along, karaoke-style, at the top of their lungs, under the impression that as they moved along, lost in their own world, no one would be able to hear it. I watched groups of school friends cycling together and chatting animatedly, heard people whistling and bells being rung. There were people cycling while also reading the morning news on their phone, and those carrying big bags, art folders, rucksacks.

I saw people ride by in smart office clothes, and construction workers in their luminous jackets. There were postmen, off to do their rounds with electric cargo bikes full of post, and one person cycling with their umbrella up. All of these sounds flew past me, and I was transfixed. Every bike that passed told a different story about how the future could be, how it could sound. Listening deeply in that way put me into a state of intense attention. Imagining that what you're listening to are the sounds of the future adds an extra layer. I also take photos in these places and then present them in my talks as precious artifacts that I have carried back from the future just for them.

Aside from harnessing the power of sound and visuals, how else might we support people in stepping out of the present and into the future? How about smell? Might we be able to help people use smell to imagine a world undergoing a 'wide-ranging, large-scale, rapid and systemic transformation'? And if we did so, might harnessing this new sense help deepen our experience? This idea that smell could itself be a time machine might not be so far-fetched.

William Tullett, in his book *Smell and the Past*, writes 'Smells are archives in miniature, they are repositories of memories and feeling.'[2] Our 'olfactory recall' can retain over ten thousand smells, to each of which we attach memories and emotions.[3] The human nose can detect one trillion odours thanks to four hundred types of scent receptors, the cells of which are renewed every thirty to sixty days.[4]

Hsuan L. Hsu, professor of English at Concordia University in Montreal, Quebec, told me, 'The power of smell might help potentially to detach us, or people, from their patterns of living.'[5] The science of smells is something that is a far bigger aspect of our lives than we may be aware of. What is known as 'scent branding' is big business. As Laurence Minsky, Colleen Fahey and Caroline Fabrigas write in the *Harvard Business Review*, 'In an age where it's becoming more and more difficult to stand out in a crowded market, you must differentiate your brand emotionally and memorably. Think about your brand in a new way by considering how scent can play a role in making a more powerful impression on your customers.'[6]

Many hotel chains, for example, spray particular scents into their lobbies or other parts of their hotels, scents unique to that brand. The Hyatt Place chain, for example, has created its own scent, called 'Seamless', described as 'fresh blueberries and light florals on a base of warm vanilla and musk'.[7] Research shows that spaces that have been 'scented' in this way can result in improved perception of product quality, increased 'purchase intent' of customers, increased duration of retail visits and greater willingness of consumers to pay more for products. They can even reduce the number of typos made by office workers.[8]

In 2013, Nissan, as part of their promotion for their LEAF electric car, hired perfumer George Dodd to create 'an aromatic blueprint of what the world could smell like in a zero-emissions (ZE) future'.[9] Inspired by the aromas of the Scottish Highlands and the desire for the scent to evoke 'clean, fresh and organic landscapes in the minds of its sniffers, designed to encourage nostalgic feelings', Dodd describes how he created his scent:

> *I start off with the cut grass – it's mixed with a delicate orange. To that I've increased the wellbeing by adding a little note of a special rose. Then I've taken the green of a coriander leaf and the lovely soothing oil from the basmati flower in India. If I mix the oils in various ratios, your unconscious recognises the feelings – the feeling of life is worth living. I want this scent of the future to really speak to your soul, to your deep unconscious, to intrigue your unconscious, and what better way for Nissan to gift this scent to its LEAF customers than in the form of a LEAF-shaped air freshener for your car.*[10]

Tullett has been very critical of Nissan's air fresheners, pointing out that the mass production of perfumes and scents in this way often involves polluting industries that can make life very unpleasant for people unlucky enough, or poor enough, to live near them.[11] Hsu pointed out to me that Nissan's idea of one single smell of the future is ridiculous anyway. After all, what is the smell of the present? Can the present be narrowed down to a single scent? What we find pleasurable in terms of smell is very culturally dependent and access to good smells is not evenly distributed. As Hsu told me, 'There's no one smell that can be the smell of the future.'[12] The smell of the present can be different with every step we take, and it would be the same for the future.

How might we do it then? While writing this book, I taught a day on imagination for forty-five students at (the now-defunct and much-missed) Schumacher College, close to where I live in Devon. After we completed the time-travel exercises described in chapter 10 (see page 143), I introduced an activity called Making Scents of the Future.[13] I told my students about the Nissan air freshener and the criticism it received. 'How would it be,' I asked, 'if we were to generate forty-five different scents of the future?' I gave each student a small paper coffee cup. 'You have 15 minutes,' I instructed, 'to create in your cup a cocktail of smells from what you can find around you that captures your idea of 2030. And, like a cocktail, you need to give it a name.'

Some went to the flower garden, some to the kitchen, some to the forest, some to the vegetable garden. When the students returned, I invited them to gather in a small part of the room, marked out on the floor by cushions, and to imagine that they were at a cocktail party in a small apartment. Their task was to circulate around the room and sniff as many of the cocktails as possible.

I joined in and enjoyed earthy smells of soil with citrus overtones, bread dough mixed with tree resin, and one that was bursting with a sense of everything green in one place. There was the subtle scent of early spring flowers. There was lavender, and there was fresh grass. Cocktail names included 'Cut Grass', 'Eucalyptus Mud Rain' and 'Fresh Futures'.

I've now done this exercise in dozens of workshops, and it is often the highlight for me. I play music, to make it feel more cocktail-party-like, and encourage people to 'work the room' and to get round the group to enjoy as many of the scents as possible rather than engaging in a long conversation about one or two of them. It is an embodiment of Rainer Maria Rilke's observation that, 'The future enters into us in this way in order to transform itself in us long before it happens.'[14] Engaging the power of smells starts to enable these futures to get inside our cells, our bones, our psyche. It's a powerful activity that stays with people for a long time afterwards.

The idea that time travel should be a multisensory experience is central to the work of Ouassima Laabich, the Berlin-based founder and lead of the project Muslim Futures, and creator of the term 'sensual futuring', which, as she writes, 'means centering questions like, "How do inclusive futures sound, taste, feel, smell. . .?"'[15] Her work is underpinned by two key questions: 'What if . . . there was such a space that allowed Muslims to draw, negotiate and envision futures worth fighting for today, futures that centre the complexity of Muslim life, that do not categorise in a racist manner, that do not criminalise Muslims and declare them the "other"? And what if we called this space "Muslim Futures"?'[16]

In her work, Ouassima asks, 'What does it mean to imagine? Who imagines? Who has the space, the capacities, the cognitive freedom to do it?' Muslim Futures uses positive futurism and time travel to explore a Muslim position that is rooted in different experiences of people from across the Muslim diaspora. In her experience, for many marginalised people, stepping into positive imagined futures is not straightforward. 'When you are busy fighting in the present(s),' she told me, 'you're busy with surviving, with fighting, with justifying, with whatever.' This led Ouassima to create interactive and participatory design futures workshops, and to her emphasising the concept of 'sensuality' in her work.

In her workshops, she integrates music and dancing, having created what she calls a 'futures playlist' for this purpose.[17] She scents the room depending on the cultural backgrounds of those attending the workshop, perhaps using citrus fruit scents, or different perfumes very popular in Muslim culture such as oud and bakhoor. She makes sure the room also has good food and teas available to people so that, as she puts it, 'the overall set-up is a sensual experience in itself'. She has also begun experimenting with touch, bringing in different textures that help people to step into the future. She adds, 'The aim is to engage the senses and co-create a moment to "forget" what was and, in order to enter the realms of imagining, what could be.'

In an article called 'On Sensual Futuring', she writes, 'In the political arena of futures thinking, imagining the unimaginable and dreaming of desirable alternatives is disruptive and becomes even more powerful if we allow for sensuality to enter the process.' Her approach expands beyond sensuality, though. As she puts it, 'Isn't the idea that we centre love, community and joy through/with sensuality both revolutionary and courageous?'[18] Her work offers insights into how we might create time machines that reshape how we approach community building and activism, something we will return to in later chapters.

This all makes me wonder if, as movements and organisations trying to change the world towards climate justice, social justice, a world doing everything it needs to do in the tiny window of time remaining, there might be tools we aren't making use of?

Let's imagine we are an organisation that has written a report – a collection of recommendations for something it wants to see happen in the world or a campaign manifesto, perhaps. We could just publish our report, put it online or hold a conference to present its key findings. Instead, what if we invited people to a banquet or cocktail party of smells? People could experience a delicious selection of scent cocktails that give them a deep sense of what the future would smell like if our proposals were to be realised. They would be able to imbibe these smells as well as perhaps make some of their own. Or, maybe people could be invited to a meal that tastes of that future? What would it taste like? What new dishes might exist? What new flavours?

Shortly, I will tell you about a group of students doing exactly that. First, I want to share the very powerful experience I had of how food and taste can break us free of the constraints of the present and allow us to experience the past through new eyes. In April 2020, I was in Brussels for a meeting of Transition activists from across Europe, and one evening, as part of the programme, an artist called Mama D Ujuaje took all forty of us on an extraordinary experience known as The Food Journey.[19]

The venue was a darkened room. Participants were blindfolded, led in and guided to our seats where Mama D and her small team transported us, using a prerecorded soundscape, to an imagined precolonial forest, inspired by West African cultures. The initial foods offered were derived from the humid tropical forest, being native and in season at the time. By following the seasons, foods can range from tiger nuts (*Cyperus esculentus*) to June plums (*Spondias mombin*) and naseberry fruit (*Manilkara zapota*), to many others.

As we ate, Mama D started the lyrical narrative that would guide us through the various stages of the journey, which began with human emergence from the forest. She then moved on to expressions of human-on-human violence, depicted by the enslavement of Africans and their trafficking to the Caribbean. While being taken through both the capture and ocean crossing, we heard and felt the weight of chains around our feet and experienced the taste of yam in our mouths – a staple food for the enslaved during these crossings.

She narrated us through our arrival in the Caribbean and the many different cultures that were assembled there over the course of three hundred years. We tasted and smelled the diverse fruits, vegetables and dishes that emerged from around the world and that became commonplace: food from Africa itself to Mesoamerica, Tahiti, Spain, India, Ireland and China, among others.

In one especially harrowing part, we heard the sounds of a verbal exchange between an enslaved person and a master overseer during an auction on a plantation, which culminated in the powerful impression of a whipping being inflicted. Mama D told us, 'It is to remind us of the implications of violence on both sides of the whip, as well as other arcs of violence between humans.'

Throughout this storytelling and soundscape, we were offered tastes and smells that connected us to that particular stage of the journey, all chosen based on her extensive research into the foods of the time. Being blindfolded, visual points of reference that keep us rooted in our present reality disappeared, set adrift in a temporal fluidity, our remaining senses accentuated.

This profound experience makes me wonder: could an experience like this – a multisensory taste-based journey through time – be designed in such a way to visit a positive future world with a similar impact on participants? I asked Mama D for her thoughts on how such an approach might be adapted for looking forward in time. She told me it's important that any such process is grounded in the life experiences of the many and diverse peoples who are rightful inheritors of a future: that ideas of the future must come from understanding how the different realities of people's presents are held and considered by those people themselves. The risk otherwise, as she puts it, is that 'it's like colonising the future. And do we want to do that again?'[20]

With these types of sensory immersive experiences, the 'pixie dust' of time travel can become even more complex, more nuanced, better resourced with tools and possibilities. Getting people to the stage of being able to say 'when I was in the future' (see Town Anywhere, chapter 5, on page 73) is more deeply impactful when we are able to include *all* the senses. As Mama D observes, 'We should not only include all of the sensory apparatus that people can respond to, but also the different ways in which the senses are connoted by different cultures. There is, as Nigerian author Chimamanda Ngozi Adichie says, a danger in a single story and so any futuring narrative needs to represent a weave of narratives arising from a diversity of experience in the present and drawn from different tellings of the past.'

In 2024, I was part of an online discussion panel with Michael Datura, principal at Cortes Island School in British Columbia, Canada.[21] Inspired by my talk of time travel and time machines, he decided to reframe the entire high school curriculum around my book *From What Is to What If.* The result was the school year culminating in what he describes as a 'time-travelling showcase'. It was held in January 2025 at the island's community centre, Mansons Hall, and transported everyone who attended to 2040. The turnout was remarkable; Michael told me, 'On an island of nine hundred, we had almost two hundred people attend.'[22]

The event was an immersive, multisensory deep dive into the intersection of art and climate, designed entirely by the students over the previous year. During that time, they explored citizen science, the ecological realities of the climate emergency and what a refocusing on resilience would mean for the people of the island.[23]

Students transformed the space into a time portal, which people entered through a beautiful, illuminated time tunnel surrounded by clocks of different sizes. Once inside, there was an art gallery of work made in 2040 and brochures from the key organisations that had enabled the island to transition to this future. These included the newly created Ministry of Beauty, an earth construction company called From the Earth, For the Earth, the fishing cooperative Future Fisheries and an ad-free social media platform called Simul that was designed to promote safer online interactions and discourage screen addiction. There were spontaneous performances, an anthology of 'What if. . .?' essays written by the students on the theme of Growing Up in the Anthropocene, and collages and sculptures showing what the island looks like in 2040.

In addition to all this, as described on the school's website:

> *Attendees were introduced to imagined scientific breakthroughs like the integration of biosonification — a technology that reads the bioelectric pulses of living organisms — with artificial intelligence (AI) to facilitate communication across species. Students also envisioned a world where education prioritizes land-based experiences, ecological awareness, and the mastery of earth-based crafts and skills, paired with Indigenous language bilingualism and mixed-grade classrooms.*[24]

The event culminated in Joanna Macy's powerful exercise 'A Council of All Beings'. Participants each took on the role of a different animal or other non-human being and made a mask to represent their creature. They then all met at a council where they discussed how the actions of human beings are impacting their existence.[25]

What stood out for me, though, was that the event also included 'futuristic food'. After considerable debate among the students about the pros and cons of insect protein, Michael told me, 'We served vegetarian finger food – the kinds you might get at an art gallery opening – with a focus on seaweed and, where possible, local ingredients. We had a local caterer arrange the food in futuristic-looking ways – essentially what you might find in "high dining". It was, importantly, all free.'[26]

Next to the food was the following text, written by one of the students:

> *In the 2040s, the living world's well-being is always considered in the food production process. Resources are used wisely,*

> *with agricultural practices designed to replenish rather than deplete the Earth's ecosystems. Vertical farming, regenerative agriculture, and aquaponics have become widespread, optimizing urban spaces and significantly reducing the need for vast tracts of land and water. Humanity has mastered sustainable food production methods that are highly efficient, require fewer inputs, and leave a minimal environmental footprint. This evolution marks a profound shift toward a future where food systems work in harmony with both human and ecological health.*[27]

Rather than just writing about the future of food in an essay, here people could actually taste it, surrounded by artefacts and stories from the future. It all makes me wonder: if you were planning futuristic food for an event, what would be on the menu? And, perhaps more importantly, how different would our education system be if every school had a principal like Michael who turned their school into a time machine?

CHAPTER EIGHT

Tell a New Story of Time

The sociologist Barbara Adam once noted that, 'Time is a most effective colonising tool.'[1] Colonising powers saw the future as something to be plundered, mined, extracted from, something fundamentally *theirs*. Their ambitions knew no limits. Cecil Rhodes, the mining magnate and politician who gave his name to Rhodesia, now Zimbabwe, wrote, 'I would annex the planets if I could. I often think of that. It makes me sad to see them so clear and yet so far.'[2]

Men like Rhodes also fell in love with the future – in their own destructive ways. But it was a future in which there was no space for the people they colonised – no consideration for their needs, their hopes and desires, no vision beyond colonisers exerting their will over the colonised. And, for a time, they succeeded. In a speech to the Colonial Institute in 1893, Foreign Minister Lord Rosebery, talking about the British colonisation of Africa, explained, 'We are engaged, in the language of mining, "in pegging out claims for the future". We have to consider not what we want now, but what we shall want in the future.'[3]

New York Times bestselling author adrienne maree brown sums it up best, more than 120 years later: 'We are living in the ancestral imagination of others, with their longing for safety and abundance, a longing that didn't include us, or included us as enemy, fright, other.'[4]

There is, in other words, a particular relationship with the past, the future and control of time for those who have been colonised, enslaved, marginalised and erased, as well as for those who did the colonising. As futurist Fred Polak wrote in 1973, 'The images of the future that man has created are intimately related to the time concepts he has held.'[5]

So many questions arise from this. Whose vision of the future is the 'right' one? How do we integrate our knowledge of violent and exploitative pasts – not to mention a violent and exploitative present – with a vision of the future that works for everyone? And how might shifting our understanding of what time is and how it works alter the activism we do and how we do it? This is a conundrum for climate activists, and one we've not addressed particularly well, for the most part.

I've had the fortune to meet and learn from people who are working at the intersection of these questions, people whose work inspires me hugely, people whose life experience is very different from mine as a white, male, cisgender, straight, able-bodied person. I find far more inspiration in the work of, for example, women of colour writing about imagination and time travel than I do in yet another narrative about collapse and extinction. What I love about their work is a freedom, a fluidity, a willingness to play with time, and the searching for new ways to talk about and understand time. They bring insights to the question of how we might best focus on the nurturing of longing that I have been seeking for a long time.

Before we go on to dive deeply into different understandings of time and why they matter so much, I want to introduce you to some of the people whose fresh thinking about time and its connection to colonisation and whose practice of 'temporal fluidity' has inspired me. An organisation called Fiveable, in an online class on performance art, gives a beautiful definition that fits so well here:

> *Temporal fluidity refers to the concept of time being experienced as flexible and dynamic rather than fixed and linear. In immersive experiences, this means that participants can engage with time in varied ways, allowing them to move through past, present, and future moments in a seamless and often non-chronological manner. This fluidity can create deeper emotional connections and enhance the overall experience by encouraging a more organic interaction with the narrative or environment.*[6]

Black Quantum Futurism

Rasheedah Phillips and Camae Ayewa live in North Philadelphia, a predominantly Black neighbourhood experiencing the pressures of gentrification, but one also described as 'home to an emerging movement of grassroots futurist practices inspired by the experiences of poor, Black, brown and queer people in the city'.[7] In 2014, Phillips, who is also a housing lawyer and Ayewa, an artist and musician who tours under the name Moor Mother, launched a project called Black Quantum Futurism, or BQF, arguing that the right to design the future has been placed into the hands of a small number of organisations and the wealthy and powerful. For people of colour it is even more complex. They are often airbrushed out of visions of the future, as well as out of memories of the past. Phillips asks, 'How does a radical movement conceive of its own future when the future was never meant for them?'[8]

BQF grew out of The AfroFuturist Affair, a grassroots organisation that created both an online and physical space for Black people to meet to explore Afrofuturism, speculative fiction and science fiction, inspired by Phillips' love of science fiction combined with her frustration at not seeing herself as a Black queer woman reflected in much of what she was reading. BQF is also inspired by Afrofuturism, which in popular culture has come to be associated with music, art, fashion and design, films like *Black Panther*, musicians such as OutKast, Parliament Funkadelic, Flying Lotus and Sun Ra, along with internet subcultures, academia and aesthetics. American singer and rapper Janelle Monáe describes Afrofuturism as 'Black people seeing ourselves in the future'.[9]

For Phillips and Ayewa, Afrofuturism goes far beyond fashion and music; it's a vehicle for radical community activism. Phillips says, 'Afrofuturism prompted me to think about alternative temporalities, how time imprints itself on communities, and how time plays out in the lives of marginalised and oppressed people who have uneven access to both their histories and their futures.'[10] She continues, 'It should increasingly be applied to other areas of study, such as law, architecture, psychology, social work, public policy, etc. I hope to see Black communities continue to take Afrofuturism and its potential seriously as a creative force for worldbuilding and worldchanging, and to develop it as such. We need Afrofuturistic Environmental Science, Afrofuturistic City Planning, Afrofuturistic Medicines, Afrofuturistic Math, Afrofuturistic Horology.'[11]

In 2016, BQF took over an empty shop in their neighbourhood and reopened it as a Community Futures Lab (CFL), hosting workshops on topics such as Design as Protest, zine-making sessions, performances of stories, poems and songs written by visitors to the Lab as well as by BQF themselves, and collecting 'oral histories, memories, alternative temporalities and futures'.[12] Outside, a sandwich board declared that 'Sci-fi is Strategy'[13] and inside, people recorded their 'oral futures' in booths with wall-mounted telephones.[14]

BQF's output includes experimental music – performances that combine Ayewa's music with Phillips' spoken-word explorations around themes of time and reimagining our relationship to it. They've produced zines, anthologies, films and sci-fi novels. They also present workshops and lectures, have been artists-in-residence at the Institute of Contemporary Art in London and the Chicago Architecture Biennial, and have won multiple awards.[15] In 2017, Phillips and Ayewa ran a programme and exhibit at the Icebox Project Space in Philadelphia called Time Camp 001, which they describe as 'A two-day program and interactive installation exploring time, alternative temporalities, time travel, and temporal shifts from various frameworks, disciplines, and cultural traditions.'[16] In 2021, BQF was selected for the 2021 European Organization for Nuclear Research's (CERN) Collide artist's residency, working alongside particle physics researchers to explore parallel observations and interpretations of time, including within the context of quantum physics. For example, Phillips and Ayewa write, 'Through the intersections of art and science, our project will explore what it would mean to understand or experience the non-linearity or subjective nature of time as part of global or local timekeeping and calendaring methods.'[17]

Their creativity, their design style, their iconography of clocks and collages of images from Black history transposed into the future, the way they combine music, spoken word and video, their whole way of talking about time travel is rooted in a belief that in order to change the world, we need to be able to imagine different futures – the futures that we long for, in ever greater clarity, so that we can then bring them back with us into the present.

Afronautic Research Labs

For the next story, imagine you walk through a door. The room inside is dark, apart from a few desk lamps pointing down onto the large table in the centre of the room. It's quiet, like a reading library. As you enter, you are handed a rectangular magnifying glass, the size of a small iPad, which has built-in lights to illuminate what you're looking at. As your eyes adjust to the light, you can see that there are other people already in the room and that the table is covered with laminated documents that the people are browsing through. There are old maps, depicting the east coast of Canada, with hatched lines leading to the east coast of Africa. The routes of slavers.

You shuffle through the other papers on the desk in front of you. There's a scan of an old poster reading: 'Public Auction. Monday, 3rd of November 1760. To be sold, at the house of Mr John Rider. Two slaves, boy and girl, about 11 years old. Halifax.' There's an advert from the classified section of a newspaper offering a ten-dollar reward for a thirty-five-year-old slave who has escaped captivity. The person posting the advert, John Turner, adds at the end, 'Whoever carries him off or employs him after this public notice, shall be prosecuted according to the Law.'[18]

There's a ship's manifest, showing one crossing from Africa to Canada in which its 'cargo' consisted entirely of children, being transported for sale as if they were inanimate objects. You read a story from the historical archive of another crossing during which free Africans liberated their kidnapped shipmates. You read that nineteen slave ships were built in Newfoundland and made many trips between Canada and the west coast of Africa, transporting 5,798 enslaved people from West Africa to the Caribbean, many to Jamaica.

You look up from the table and realise that there are two people, a Black woman and a younger Black man, standing in the room, silently watching your experience. They are wearing ceremonial robes, white turbans, dark glasses with lights on the corners, and hold circular LED lights that can be used to illuminate the texts.[19] They give you a silent greeting, touching their right hands to their hearts. They are the Afronauts. They are here to witness you as you witness. Turns out, they've actually travelled back from the future just to witness this moment.

This Afronautic Research Lab is the work of Canadian artist and scholar Camille Turner, whose work combines Afrofuturism and archival research into Canada's mostly forgotten role in the slave trade.[20] Afronautic Research Labs was first performed in 2016 in Toronto and has since been performed in other Canadian cities including Montreal and Vancouver. It was inspired by a journey Camille took to Senegal, intending to use the trip to reflect on a future in which people of African descent are fully able to define their own lives. She visited sites associated with the historical slave trade and later wrote, 'At every turn on this visit to Senegal, I was reminded that I must venture into the past to gather what I need for the future.' Turner writes that while visiting a slave holding cell in Senegal, 'I realised that my ancestors may have stood in this very place, and that just as I was imagining them, they may have imagined me. I am here. I have returned. I am listening.'[21]

The role of the Afronauts, the time travellers, is what lifts this experience from being merely an informative browse of some archival material into something quite different. Camille tells me that their role (one of them is usually her) is 'to witness people witnessing their own histories', whether they are people of colour or not.

In the storytelling Camille weaves around the project, the Afronauts are related to the Dogon people of Mali whose folklore holds that they are descendants of the Nomos people from Sirius B, a star. As Camille tells it, 'You can't see Sirius B with the naked eye, and of course they didn't have telescopes, and Western scientists could not verify the presence of Sirius B until they invented the Hubble telescope.' According to the story, the Afronauts emigrated to Sirius B and have now returned to Earth after 10,000 years, because 'they realised the Earth is in trouble, we're in trouble, so they've come home to save the planet'.

I was especially interested in what it feels like to play the role of someone who has travelled from the future to bear witness to the present. 'There's something so profound about holding the space and being a witness,' she told me. I asked her what the instructions are that she gives to the people who join her to play the role of an Afronaut. 'I ask them to be there. To just be. What we are symbolising is Black people in the future . . . us not just surviving but thriving . . . and being the vehicle through which the Earth will be saved. It's a powerful stance and a powerful sort of idea to embody.'

I asked her how she thinks about time, and the philosophy of temporal fluidity that runs through her work. 'There's a simultaneity of time,' she told me. 'I think about [the future] as a place of liberation. If I anchor myself to that possible place, to that idea, then I'm able to go into painful archives and know that I will be able to come out, that there's somewhere to go.' She added, 'Understanding the past is really what people need in order to think about how to go into the future.'

What immediately attracted me to Camille's work was her playfulness with time to access and find new understandings of intensely painful historical memories. How can finding new ways to relate to the future help us understand the past? Might temporal fluidity and the kind of playfulness embodied in Afronautic Research Labs also give us new tools for living with and supporting each other through the traumas and marginalisation that so many people are also experiencing in the present day?

Germany is home to another self-identified time traveller. Promona Sengupta is an artist, academic, activist, curator and time traveller. Originally from India, she lives and works in Berlin. She is also captain and chef of what she describes as 'the interspecies intergalactic FLINTAQ+ crew of the Spaceship Beben, a deeep space exploration vehicle surfing the wonky waves of the spacetime continuum'.[22] The Spaceship Beben, Promona writes, 'flies at the edges of believability and logic, out of the imposed worlds of capitalism, patriarchy, heteronormativity, white supremacy, towards the good life'.[23]

For Promona (aka Captain Pro), time – and how we talk about it – is inherently political and of particular importance to marginalised people. Critical of most existing time-travelling stories as being 'light-hearted temporal tourism' or 'make-believe colonial adventures of time travel', she and the rest of her crew instead see time travel as a practice 'to be embarked on by those who have fallen out of time'.[24]

'Given that time travel is not the easiest of practices, given that it is engineered from the deep pain of impending death or erasure, of being out of time, out of body; given that it is the stuff of making dreams come alive, it demands a particularly strong basic ingredient – the primal erotic instinct for survival,'[25] she explains.

When I caught up with Promona via Zoom, she explained that being part of the crew of the Beben is about helping each other 'survive the wear and tear of living under patriarchy, living under capitalism, living under class, poverty, and the big structural underpinnings of this timeline . . . Time travel is a practice that we do. Space travel is a practice that we do.'

She added, 'What are our experiences in our own lives of time and space? As FLINTAQ+[26] people we are asked to not take up space. We are asked to be very small. As FLINTAQ+ people the imaginations of space that we are given don't have us in them.'

Promona explains that the Spaceship Beben engages in a creative practice around trauma, complex PTSD, flashback symptoms and other forms of time-based disorientation, in the experiences of oppressed peoples forced to survive myriad forms of violence in this world. I asked how someone can join the crew of the Beben. 'The only requirement of being on board . . . is to be able to see it,' she explained.

One of the central ideas around the Beben is believability. Promona told me that for many marginalised people, their experience is that when something traumatic happens to them and they give testimony about it, they are often put in a position where they have to prove they are telling the truth, the onus being on them to make people believe that what they say happened did actually happen. Each member of the crew has a different imagining of what the Spaceship Beben actually looks like. To Promona it appears as a 'pillow fortress' with a very specific kind of recessed lighting; to another crew member it appears as an angler fish. As for how one becomes the captain, she told me, 'I was recruited by the ship.'

Once a year, the crew meet up in person during the summer. 'We do a landing every year,' Promona tells me. 'We land together for a shore leave. Mostly on this planet. Because it's got the best food.' The gatherings take place around water. 'We have to gather around water because of the gravitational pull of this planet. You cannot land a spaceship on land. You have to land on water. We gather around water and we go swimming. We do antigravity exercises in the water. We just train and we hang out.' The event is not open to the public, just to crew and potential new recruits. What's the interview process like for becoming a new crew member, I wondered? 'We go for a swim, we come back, we have a conversation. We go for another swim. We come back. We have a conversation. It is a very long conversation.' The interview takes place in the water because 'water is the best material means to be in another world on this planet', she tells me.

In her writings, Promona sets out a very different motivation for time travel than H.G. Wells' colonial-era time traveller. 'It is convenient to believe that time travel is mere fantasy, when one has not experienced being out of time or felt the intense survival instinct of needing to be in rhythm, in presence, in one's body. For us, the chronically sick, time travel is not the imagined tourism of hopping through the Palaeolithic era, observing the pyramids under construction, meeting our descendants in flying cars, all through the wide-eyed techno-capitalist self-actualization of colonial science-fiction authors. For us, it is survival.'[27]

◆ ◆ ◆

Having met these brilliant activists whose work is rooted in an exploration of different understandings of time, specifically how time can be a tool for liberation just as much as it was used as a key tool for colonisation and oppression, it's worth taking a deeper dive into how Western understandings of time came to be and what other cultural understandings of time can teach us.

In 1687, Sir Isaac Newton wrote, 'Absolute time and mathematical time, of itself, and from its own nature, flows equally without relation to anything external.'[28] In other words, every second is uniform, every hour, every day, it all 'flows equally'. Tick, tick, tick. For Newton, time flowed, unstopping, in a linear direction, one way only, from distant past to past, from past to present, from present to future, and on into the distant future. Every tick of the clock is of the same duration whoever you are and wherever you are, and we travel along this path until, as it were, our own time runs out.

Yet Newton's absolutist concept of time bears little relation to most people's lived experience. One definition I like describes time as 'nature's way to keep everything from happening at once'.[29] Robert E. Ornstein, author of the 1969 book *On the Experience of Time*, argues that there are many kinds of time. He describes, 'The time of the poet, the philosopher, the physicist, the psychologist, the biologist, the times of the sundial, the calendar, the time to boil rice, the time of the hourglass. Time is each of these and more.'[30] A minute when our favourite football team is winning is different from a minute when they're losing. A minute in the dentist's chair feels longer than a minute at the beach.

Ornstein concedes that, at the end of a book-length exploration attempting to understand the nature of time, 'We have gone through all this to find we cannot answer it. Time is too diverse a concept to be amenable to our answer.'[31] Individual experiences of time are shaped by class, economics, race, gender and more. Indeed, some cultures throughout history have understood time in profoundly different ways to that which dominates the world today.

'Although it's true that one of these ways of thinking about time has cultural dominance, it's also not true that it has total dominance. And I find there to be something hopeful about the fact that, actually we do retain the ability to speak these other languages of time. And also, all you have to do is hang out with a three-year-old to have a different way of thinking about time,' remarked author, artist and educator Jenny Odell in a 2023 interview.[32] Whenever I've spent time in what we might called 'transitional' spaces – being present at a birth or a death – it's felt like being in a timeless space; day and night become irrelevant, time feels meaningless.

All of this makes me wonder: how did people experience time before colonisers arrived with their clocks and imposed this standard, as part and parcel of imposing control? John Mbiti, a Kenyan-born Christian philosopher, describes how African peoples in a traditional way of life perceive time – what he calls the 'African time concept'.

> *For them, time is simply a composition of events which have occurred, those which are taking place now and those which are immediately to occur. What has not taken place or what has no*

> *likelihood of an immediate occurrence falls in the category of 'No-time'. What is certain to occur, or what falls within the rhythm of natural phenomena, is in the category of inevitable or potential time.*[33]

In this sense, time is seen as having a very long past, a present, and a very short and limited future. Because the future hasn't happened yet, it therefore cannot be described as time, Mbiti argues, and once something happens, it becomes the present before rapidly moving into the past. The past, the present and things in the immediate future that we know are going to happen can be explained as time because, as Mbiti puts it, 'Time has to be experienced in order to make sense or to become real.'[34] In this way, time moves backwards, rather than forwards. Things happen in the present, and then they move backwards into the past. In a linguistic analysis of the Kikamba and Gikuyu languages, Mbiti discovered that there are no verb tenses for anything more than six months in the future.

Mbiti's work has subsequently been criticised by several scholars. Jonathan Alabi of the University of Lagos argues that 'it would be false to conclude that these two ethnic groups form a definitive base for all African tribal thought',[35] and points to other tribal groups who he argues have a very clear sense of the future. Joseph Ekong identifies traditional practices of food storage, perennial farming and divination as pointing to a clear notion of the future, writing, 'The African consciousness of *future time* is clearly manifested in various ways.'[36] However, Alabi adds, 'There is still something magnificently beautiful, admirable and relevant in Mbiti's concept of time,'[37] and his work is still cited as an inspiration by Afrofuturists and by activists such as Black Quantum Futurism.

One of those who takes inspiration from Mbiti's approach is Nikitah Okembe-RA Imani, artist and professor and former chair of Black studies at the University of Nebraska-Omaha. He told me, referring to Mbiti's work, that there are two Swahili words denoting very different experiences of time: 'Sasa' time and 'Zamani' time. Sasa time represents an expanded concept of 'now', what we feel to be current, what we feel our present time consists of. Anything more than six months into the future, he told me, is not Sasa time. In order to qualify as Sasa, it needs to be about to happen, to be happening now or to have just occurred. A community can also have its own Sasa, which is longer than the individual's. We might think of it as 'micro time'. When people die, it is believed they remain as part of Sasa time for as long as there are still people alive who remember their name.

Zamani, on the other hand, is what we might call 'macro time'. It is ultimately where everything ends up, where everything that ever happened can still be found – 'the eternal', if you like, or 'the final storehouse of time in which everything becomes absorbed into a reality that is neither after nor before'.[38] Zamani is alive with myth, with characters and stories that are far more important as a source of learning and wisdom than the future. For Imani, Zamani and Sasa are 'two giant circles that we're all on . . . You constantly have to stay in touch with your material existence, and then you have your . . . eternal spiritual sky existence . . . we are small circles that are part of a big circle . . . a circular and cyclical notion of time as opposed to the conveyor belt [model].'

This way of understanding time represents a profound difference from the idea that time moves inexorably in one direction towards dissolution. Imani told me, 'There's an elder who told me one time "you build for eternity". Just think about [that] as opposed to building for financial gain right now, fame, fortune. This notion that as an artist, for example . . . what I create from the very beginning I conceive as eternal. Or something that would be worthy of eternal existence. That's going to change the nature of the painting I create!'

For Imani, this means that 'all three dimensions in a sense exist simultaneously. You *are* the past. You're not simply descended from your ancestors: you *are* the present-day manifestation of them. People say, "How come African people can't get over slavery?" I say, "You don't understand: I *can't* get over it. It's *me*. And, literally, my grandmother was a child on a slave plantation. That's how close it is. My parents went through segregation. What you're talking about getting past is *me*!" . . . You *are* your ancestors.

'In fact, in many African languages, when you introduce yourself, you don't say "I'm glad to be here"; the equivalent would be "*We* are glad to be here". There's the me, the temporal me that you know as me, the self, the individual. But there's the eternal me, which is the continuation of that larger cycle and everything that I am is a reflection in many ways of that. I'm bringing my ancestors – they're with me, they're in me – with me, as well as my future progeny. We're all there. It's crowded in the room!'

Given that there have been, and still are, so many different ways of understanding time, including the two mentioned above, how has one become so dominant? Clocks and hourly bells became a fixture of colonisation. As historian Giordano Nanni writes, 'a functioning clock became more than an instrument of conquest . . . it was also a symbol of civilisation'.[39] This model of time, coupled with a drive to 'transcend the limits of nature', became indivisible from 'progress' and 'civilisation', and a key aspect of the colonial project around the world. As Nanni puts it, 'The more a society was considered to be "civilised", the greater the extent to which its calendars, discourses and computations of time were "reckoned without reference to any of the factors given by nature".'[40]

While clocks drove a sense of uniformity, the time people actually set those clocks to was initially anything but. As James Gleick puts it, 'All time was local time.'[41] The first people to implement uniform time zones were US railroad companies. It is said that if you travelled from Washington to San Francisco by train in the 1870s, you would need to reset your watch over two hundred times.[42] In 1884, governments from twenty-five countries met in Washington DC for the Prime Meridian Conference, where they agreed that Greenwich should be the prime meridian, in effect making it the centre of the world. The time set by the Royal Observatory at Greenwich and the Electric Time Company was distributed around the country via telegraph signals.

The relationship between time and colonisation is important to explore here. As Nanni writes, 'Clocks, it is often forgotten, do not keep *the* time, but *a* time.'[43] Imposing Western time on cultures around the world hastened the erasure of language and traditions. For example, when Europeans in the 'New World' (new to them at least) described cultures they perceived as having no sense of time, they used it to establish otherness, and as Charles Marie de La Condamine noted in 1745, having described how, in his opinion, Indigenous Americans had no language to express 'time' or 'duration', or 'virtue', 'justice', 'liberty', 'discourse' or 'ingratitude', he went on to refer to 'the little progress which the spirit of these people has made'.[44] In Australia, Western descriptions of Indigenous peoples as 'timeless' were cited in land claims by European settlers. Historian Dipesh Chakrabarty has said that, 'History is a temporality backed by superior firepower.'[45]

This colonisation of time, this widespread adoption of a model of time designed to serve capital and markets, lies behind many of the forces that reduce humanity's capacity to connect to positive futures. One of the ways it shows up is in 'time poverty'. While economic activity around the world has more or less steadily increased, it has not led to our having more time; in fact, quite the opposite. Time poverty has been defined as 'the chronic feeling of having too many things to do and not enough time to do them in'.[46]

You are likely familiar with what time poverty feels like. It makes us more miserable, more anxious, more depressed, more stressed. It means we laugh less, exercise less and make less healthy choices around food. It makes it more likely that we will get divorced, and that we'll get sick more often. The burden of time poverty falls largely on the shoulders of the poorest and most marginalised in society, people of colour, and on women and caregivers.[47] It's very hard to plan for the future, never mind fall in love with it, when you're just about managing day-to-day.

To live with a different relationship with time is very difficult when everything, from the phones in our pockets to our plans for our days are dictated to the minute by one model of time. The idea that we could live our lives thinking differently about time can feel impossible, and if you were to stop right now and ask anyone sat near you as you're reading this, they would almost certainly tell you that it's impossible too. But if unlocking the longing required to transform the world with historically unprecedented urgency requires us to find a new story of time, then perhaps we need to start by reflecting on what we mean by 'impossible' anyway? Perhaps the problem with all of this is that we accept, rather than challenge, what we believe to be possible and impossible?

CHAPTER NINE

From the Impossible to the Not Yet

In 1963, Russia and the United States were deep in the 'space race' to be the first to set foot on the Moon. Billions of dollars were invested, and the United States eventually won. Meanwhile, in Zambia, a man called Edward Mukuka Nkoloso had different ideas. He had just founded the Zambian National Academy of Science, Space Research and Philosophy, telling the world's press, 'I see the Zambia of the future as a space-age Zambia, more advanced than Russia or America. In fact, in my Academy of Science, our thinking is already six or seven years ahead of both powers.'[1]

Nkoloso had been a teacher and a fighter in the Zambian war of independence before embarking on his space project. He solicited $7 million from UNESCO and $1.9 billion from 'private foreign sources', none of whom deigned to reply to him. He took over an abandoned farm eleven kilometres from Zambia's capital of Lusaka and turned it into his Afronaut training centre. He assembled his team, consisting of twelve young men and a young woman called Marta Mwambwa, who was to be his space traveller.

Nkoloso was secretive about his rocket designs, and suspicious that Russian and American spies would try to steal his plans. He argued that one way the Zambian government could help would be with 'detention without trial for spies'. We don't know much about his actual rocket, called Cyclops 1, but in a news piece for ITV filmed at the time, his rocket appears to be a simple aluminium tube about one metre tall. A newspaper headline from the time announced: 'Rocket a Bit Wobbly.'

In a news report from 1964, Nkoloso said, 'I'll have my first Zambian astronaut on the Moon by 1965. My spacemen are ready, but we're having a few difficulties. We are using my own firing system, derived from the catapult.'[2] When it became clear that the catapult system wasn't going to work, Nkoloso began describing his plans for 'turbulent propulsion'[3] instead.

Nkoloso was ambitious. He also planned a mission to Mars. In an article called 'We're Going to Mars! With a Spacegirl, Two Cats and a Missionary' he wrote, 'I have warned the missionary he must not force Christianity on the people of Mars if they do not want it.'[4] The training his Afronauts underwent on the abandoned farm included being rolled down a hill in an empty oil drum to simulate the disorientating effects of space travel, and being swung on a rope and then, when the swinging person reached the maximum height, cutting the rope so they experienced a moment of weightlessness (before, presumably, falling and hurting themselves quite badly). They also had to learn to walk on their hands as that was, he said, 'the only way humans can walk on the Moon'.

By late 1965, the Zambian Space Programme had unravelled. As you probably noticed, they didn't make it to the Moon or Mars, but it wasn't a failure either. In a newly independent nation, Nkoloso had created a 'utopian moment', a temporary Wakanda, a place where Zambians could be whatever they wanted to be. A place with no limits. In 1989, when he died, Nkoloso was buried with the highest honours Zambia could give its citizens – a hero's burial.

Nkoloso believed that Zambia could become 'controllers of the seventh heaven of interstellar space'. He argued that Zambia was just as capable of getting to the Moon as the United States, Russia or any other country. He wasn't worried about being declared ridiculous. The Zambian Space Programme was not a joke. Nkoloso always wore, for no obvious reason, a red cape. He was an 'everyday utopian', and an extraordinary storyteller.

I share Edward Mukuka Nkoloso's story here because I think there's a lot we can learn from it. All organisations, local and national governments, oil and gas companies, arms manufacturers, insurers, banks, businesses, everyone, need urgently to master the great art of temporal fluidity, to have the courage to release the kind of deep reimagining that the climate emergency and other interconnected crises demand, to bring a new story of the future alive, one they'll be happy to hand on to their grandchildren. They need the courage to do things widely believed to be impossible, but which we know to be the only possible way to preserve a viable human presence on this planet. We need companies, local governments, everyone who can influence or change anything, to be a lot more like Edward Mukuka Nkoloso, to playfully model what it looks like to act is if the impossible is, actually, possible.

As the great jazz artist and pioneer of Afrofuturism (before it was called Afrofuturism) Sun Ra once said, 'The impossible attracts me, because everything possible has been done and the world didn't change.'[5] This concept of the impossible appears often in Black history and activism. Nannie Helen Burroughs was one of a group of Black women who started and led schools for Black women and girls around the turn of the twentieth century, with, as American writer and professor emeriti Audrey Thomas McCluskey puts it, roots in 'strong religious convictions, belief in Black women's leadership as a key to racial progress, and maternal love for the schools they founded'.[6]

Burroughs founded the National Training School for Women and Girls, which opened in Washington DC in 1909, the first all-female school to open outside of the Deep South to be run by a Black woman. She once said, 'We specialise in the wholly impossible.'

This concept, that we need to shift our focus to the impossible, is also argued by Slovenian philosopher and cultural theorist Slavoj Žižek, who writes, 'At certain levels, things we think of as possible are certainly not possible: all those dreams of immortality or whatever. And at certain levels, what economists are telling us is impossible is possible. The impossible happens: not impossible in the sense of religious miracles, but in the sense of something we don't consider possible within our coordinates . . . The only realistic option is to do what appears within this system. This is how the impossible becomes possible.'[7] Every story I shared in chapter 4 will have been dismissed as 'impossible' in its early days, until the organisers proved otherwise. As the students in Paris during the student revolution of 1968 used to say, 'Be realistic. Demand the impossible.'[8]

Which brings us back to the great Sun Ra. An extraordinary artist, Ra told a story about himself that he wasn't a human being at all, rather he was an angel from Saturn. He used space travel as a way of talking about Black liberation, which was different to many other movements at the time.[9] Sun Ra biographer William Sites wrote that Ra did what he did with 'both unshakable certainty and deadpan humour'.[10] An approach I suspect is emulated by many of the time travellers I have already introduced you to, myself included.

Sites describes Ra as a practitioner of 'everyday utopianism'.[11] When I asked John Corbett, writer and Ra archivist and scholar, if Ra actually believed he was from Saturn, he said:

> *Not only do I think he believed it, I believe it. . . whatever the answer is in terms of how one feels about his use of and his story about his extraterrestriality, Sun Ra was very serious*

about what he did, and he spent his entire life doing it. There wasn't an offstage/onstage persona. For me that is evidence of someone whose overall project is not a theatrical project, it's one that takes very seriously the question of identity and reality.

As an 'everyday utopian', Ra and all of his band, Sun Ra Arkestra (many of whom lived together in the same house), always dressed in their extraordinary space costumes, even when going to the launderette. (One reviewer, who saw the Arkestra play in 1983, described them as being 'like watching a nativity play where everyone has decided to be one of the three kings'.[12]) This was not a stage persona; it was who they were. Sites makes a useful distinction between utopian 'projects' and utopian 'moments'. The purpose of a utopian *project*, he says, is 'to imagine a world that is just, and to render its workings in sufficient detail as to make such a place compelling enough to inspire action in pursuit of its realization'.[13] It's dreaming big, setting out clear, detailed visions of distant utopias, like the utopian experiments of the interwar years and the 1960s.

Utopian *moments* on the other hand refers to commonplace, everyday utopian moments in which the present 'overflows with what is not yet',[14] providing tastes, glimpses, infusions of utopias, of ideal futures in the present, whether through music, art, activist events – all manner of creative expressions of the utopian urge. Many of the stories I've told you up to this point are utopian 'moments' rather than utopian 'projects'.

Unlike utopian 'projects', which tend to be the reserve of 'experts', Sites told me:

There's something deeply democratic about the idea of utopian moments, which are available to all of us. They may afford opportunities for sudden glimpses that the world could be quite different from the way it is, that there are certain things

> *that may even be in our world, that point to a different kind of place, where we would like to live, where we would like to be . . . These are deeply sustaining moments, both for political activists but also just for ordinary folk who are not trying simply to survive a day but to experience a day which has moments of release, of joy, of celebration, and of the capacity to envision a different kind of world.*[15]

For example, in the 1970s, shortly after Ra and the Arkestra moved to Philadelphia, and just days after he had told percussionist James Jacson that he needed a new drum, a tree opposite their shared house on Morton Street was hit by lightning. Ra suggested Jacson turn part of the fallen tree into a drum. The drum Jacson created, christened by Ra the Ancient Egyptian Infinity Lightning and Thunder Drum, became a central part of their stage show for many years.

Fast forward fifty years to a beautiful late-September day in 2021in Philadelphia, where the Arkestra still live and perform (Ra himself passed away in 1993 but the Arkestra plays on). People are arriving at the city's Awbury Arboretum with a sense of great anticipation. The day feels festive. They bring picnic blankets and camping chairs, and enter the meadow at the arboretum's heart from various different paths. There's a stage set up in front of a beautiful stand of trees, covered in saplings and artistically arranged branches. In an adjoining grove of trees, speakers have been set up, playing recordings of sounds of Saturn, created by an artist who works at NASA. People are making leaf prints, and children of all ages and their mothers arrive carrying satchels containing tree seedlings. They are all here for the event called 'Summoning the Future Forest'.

From the top of the meadow, the Arkestra arrive, emerging from the trees looking resplendent, among them the band's then ninety-seven-year-old band leader Marshall Allen. They process with great pageantry towards the stage, playing 'Calling Planet Earth'. They play their set of extraordinary music through a giant sound system.[16]

The invitation to the event stated: 'Join us for a participatory intra-galactic forest performance crafted to summon the forces of the galaxy to seed a future forest for Philadelphia.' It also said that the Arkestra's performance 'will set in motion a sonic summoning of cosmic frequencies conjuring a future canopy'.[17] Those attending are invited to help make new drums from trees that had fallen in the arboretum and to play them as part of their experience, continuing Jacson's tradition.

This event was part of a larger project by S(tree)twork, an offshoot of the Pennsylvania Horticultural Society, which aims to respond to the climate emergency by galvanising communities through 'cultural activism' to create more urban forests, especially in what are termed 'low tree canopy neighbourhoods', usually poorer Black and Brown communities. The city's urban forest is in decline, just at the very time when people urgently need the cooling and shade-creating powers of trees.

What if 'Summoning the Future Forest' turned out to actually do just that? What if the future that we need to see is only going to happen if we do summon it, if we create the opportunities for people to experience and connect with that future? Perhaps, one day, people will look back and say that that glorious event, that utopian moment, actually *did* summon the future forest, actually drew it back from the future and into the present?

Already, it has led to the planting of many new trees in poorer neighbourhoods in the city. As part of those tree-planting events, residents were invited to help plant trees, and to make and play drums, while accompanied by percussionists playing the drums that have already been constructed. If the Arkestra and everyone who joined them in the meadow that day are able to generate sufficient longing to summon a future forest, what else might our collective longing be able to summon?

In September 2024, as I was working on the manuscript for this book, I travelled to Copenhagen in Denmark for two days of workshops and talks. One of the highlights was an evening talk I gave at the City Hall, a beautiful old building run by the city administration in the centre of the city.[18] For this evening, I thought I would try something a little different, a twist on the practices set out in this book so far, with the ideas and stories from its pages still running around my head after a read-through of the manuscript on the long train ride to Denmark.

Rather than ushering the audience straight into the room to take their seats, we asked them to remain in the large hallway outside, as Ruth Ben-Tovim and I had done two weeks earlier when we ran Ruth's Town Anywhere exercise in Bristol (see Town Anywhere, chapter 5, page 73). When the time came for the event to begin, with the anticipation palpable, I went out of the doors into the hallway, stood on a bench and asked the two hundred or so people waiting there to huddle in close so they could hear me.

I told them that they had the most incredible good fortune because this evening, for one night only, we had succeeded in turning this beautiful old room into a time portal. I had brought with me my time machine (actually . . . shhhh . . . my small wooden box with a pink light in it). I told them I had, along with my crack team of time engineers, managed to access a quantum thread into the future. This would mean that when they stepped through the doors into the room, they would, in reality, be stepping into the 2030 that is the result of our doing absolutely everything we could have possibly done during that time. There was laughter, but at the same time, people were transfixed, captivated, curious. Might the impossible perhaps, just perhaps, actually be possible?

Moving to stand next to the huge, ornate old doors that led into the room, I told everyone that when stepping through into 2030 they may well experience the air feeling different, the light looking a little different, and to be prepared for the sensations that would inevitably accompany stepping through a time portal that takes them six years into the future. I told them this was a process that would impact them on a quantum level, but I reassured them that any effects would be short-lived. I then got everyone to join me in counting up through the years, '2024, 2025, 2026' and so on. When we reached '2030!', the doors opened and everyone slowly entered, in silence, while music played and they found their seats.[19] It was a magical moment.

Once seated, I asked the time travellers to close their eyes and take a walk around the Copenhagen of 2030, and for two minutes to explore its streets and parks using all their senses. You could have heard a pin drop. I then called them back to the present and invited anyone who wanted to share their impressions to do so. Hands went up. People described a future that was greener, quieter, with fewer cars, more trees, more meaningful work, less stress and improved mental health, louder birdsong, a more caring community. It's like this pretty much every time I do this exercise. No one ever has ever said, with a frisson of pride, 'We've got a new IKEA that's four times bigger than the one we had five years ago.'

It reminded me of Elise Boulding's words, as discussed in chapter 2, 'We have many more potential co-workers in the task of building a more peaceful world than we ever knew.'[20] Indeed, in 2024, the results of a representative survey in 125 countries, based on interviews with nearly 13,000 people, showed widespread support for climate action. Of the world's population, 69 per cent would be willing to contribute 1 per cent of their income to addressing the climate emergency. Furthermore, 86 per cent supported pro-climate social norms. And 89 per cent supported the demand for greater political action. These figures were especially high in the countries whose citizens are more vulnerable to the impacts of climate change.

Another important finding, however, was that, 'Individuals around the world systematically underestimate the willingness of their fellow citizens to act. This perception gap . . . poses challenges to further climate action.'[21] What's missing is not public support then, but maybe a life-affirming narrative that people feel excited about and included in? Something to run towards rather than run screaming from in the opposite direction?

That evening in City Hall, I described to everyone one of my recent trips to 2030, showing them photos and playing them field recordings from that future. I told them a thrilling tale of a future in which oil and gas companies had gone out of business and renewable energy had taken up the slack, much of the new infrastructure of renewables in community ownership, with the benefits now visible for all to see. The following morning, Jacob Rask, one of the event organisers, showed me a news article on his phone.

Much to everyone's surprise, a report by Denmark's Chamber of Advocates exposed that, for the past thirty-four years, the Danish government's practice of awarding oil and gas licences in Danish waters had been illegal. According to press reports, this legal about-face could lead to the revocation of many oil and gas licences and, effectively, an end to the extraction of oil and gas in Danish waters.[22]

That same morning, in the UK, an historic High Court decision reversed approval of a hugely controversial new coal mine in Cumbria, the first new deep coal mine in over thirty years. The company behind the mine had argued it would have a 'broadly neutral effect on the global release of greenhouse gas' (a remarkable thing for anyone opening a new coal mine to say with a straight face) and one the High Court judge dismissed as 'legally flawed'.[23] The case was brought by Friends of the Earth and by South Lakes Action on Climate Change (SLACC), the local Transition group. Maggie Mason of SLACC told the BBC, 'This groundbreaking judgement could advance the global phase-out of fossil fuels. It is that big.'[24]

Jacob and I excitedly shared these stories, reflecting that perhaps they represented a shift we will look back on as the long-awaited tipping point that began to unravel the oil and gas industry. 'What have we done?' Jacob asked. We wondered whether perhaps our interfering with time the previous evening and twice already that day, that deep-level quantum tinkering had, in fact, somehow torn the fabric of time itself, and things that weren't supposed to happen for ten years or so, were somehow being dragged back into the present. Impossible? Maybe. . .

Perhaps, we reflected out loud as we digested these two huge developments, through this work, this 'temporal fluidity', sprinkling the pixie dust of time travel, we had found a way to accelerate change. Might it be that thanks to our detailed work on time travel and the creation of magical events, as well as to my small wooden box with its bright pink light, we had found a way to hack this, to make the 'impossible' tangible and manifest in the present moment? I'm not trying to suggest that these breakthroughs arose from anything other than incredibly hard work by legal experts and climate activists. But it was thrilling, nonetheless. Perhaps that moment was what it felt like to live through what, with hindsight, we will come to recognise as having been a tipping point?

That's the thing with tipping points, you can only see them in the rear-view mirror, with the benefit of hindsight. The kind of transformed, far lower carbon, more just, equal and exciting future that we've discussed here will only result from unprecedentedly effective collective action, from blocking the things that are pushing the world over the edge while building the systems and the infrastructure that come next, from resistance and skilful organising, all the while supporting each other in doing so.

It won't happen by magic. But perhaps it can be accelerated, brought forward, if we can find those ways to rend the fabric of time, to release the hold the present has over us, to release our certainty of linear time. If we can master the art of time travel, become adept sprinklers of pixie dust, help people experience stepping into the near future and bring it back with us as we did that night in Copenhagen, perhaps we might be able to accelerate things in as-yet unimaginable ways. As I asked in chapter 3, what would our activism look like if we acted as though time travel was possible?

Isn't that what the real magic of the story of Edward Mukuka Nkoloso is – how he managed to tell a story so ambitious, so huge, so ridiculous, so impossible, but with such unshakeable conviction and belief, that it expanded people's sense of what might actually be possible, what they might be capable of? He reached forward through time and pulled into the present a future that looked very different from the present and asked people, 'Why not?' Let's replace the word 'impossible' with 'not yet' and see where it goes.

CHAPTER TEN

A Time Machine Blueprint

As you approach the end of this book, I'd like to offer you a gift that I hope will be one of the most precious things you could possess at this moment in history: an actual time machine. Or rather, I'm going to give you the blueprints, the plans for *my* time machine. You will no doubt add to my plans, experiment, find new and wonderful ways of opening time portals, add incredible new technologies that I've not yet thought of, and together we will advance these tools in new and surprising ways. This is a powerful device. Use it wisely.

The first thing to say is that it's often best not to just dive into time travel. People need to warm up a little first, to engage their imaginations. One way I do that is to put people into pairs and tell them that I will shortly be showing them an object. They will have one and a half minutes to think of as many alternative uses for that object as they can. There are no right answers. They don't have to be thinking, 'Could I take this idea on *Dragons' Den*?' The idea is just to throw out ideas. They don't have to write them down, but they should keep a count of how many they come up with.

Then I show them the object. It could be a paper coffee cup, sometimes it's my shoe or sometimes it's an unusual object I've spotted in the room that I think would be good for this exercise.

I say 'go!' and when the time is up, participants shout out their best ideas.

We then move on to the time machine. This is an exercise I've used and honed over the years, but no doubt you will adapt and tweak it and come up with something better. Take this and evolve it, make it your own, add new things. I've done this exercise with groups of anywhere between 10 and 1,500, and while the core exercise remains the same, there are a few tricks I've learned that really help it to work. Firstly then, here are a few key elements for how to build an effective time machine.

Make It Theatrical

When I do my time-travel activity, I usually start with a preamble about how we are going to make history, that you will be able to tell your grandchildren you were here at the first ever act of time travel in the history of [insert name of place]. I tell them that in my hometown of Totnes, we have built the world's first time machine, but that since Brexit, getting an export licence to move it around is tricky. So, our team have gone on to invent another version that can transform any space into a time machine. I insist that that gets an 'ooh' from the audience – I mean, that is pretty impressive, right? Play up what an incredible experience they are about to have and what your credentials are as their guide. (Like Andy Clee on page 86 in chapter 5, you might want to tell them you're only recently qualified.) I then unveil, with a flourish, my 'time machine', a small box that contains an Aputure light (a very bright LED light that can be set to any colour you like), which I slowly open as though it was the most extraordinary invention ever (which it is), inviting another 'ooh'. If you can get the venue to dim the lights at the moment you open the box, it can create a magical visual experience. Of course, your time machine may look like something completely different from mine.

Put People into Pairs

This is a trick I learned through practise. Time travel is an exercise you want people to take seriously, to participate in fully and not undermine by giggling and messing around. People need to feel safe in suspending disbelief. Ask people to make a pair with someone they didn't know when they arrived. You need to then give the room a minute or so to rearrange itself. People will be wondering why you've done it, so I always say, 'Sociologists say we live in an "epidemic of loneliness". Well, by doing this, even if tonight turns out to be the worst talk you ever attended, you will at least know one person you didn't know when you came here, and that's really important.' I also tell them that having done this at the start of my presentations for many years, I have had four couples come up to me subsequently and tell me that this was how they met. And one had a baby. 'So be careful,' I tell the audience. The reason for their being in pairs will become clear after the time travelling.

Set the Scene

Next, you will need something that marks the transition from the present day to the future time. This is very important: you need tricks that allow people to feel as though they are being picked up from the present and taken elsewhere, stepping across a threshold. I have three different ways of doing this depending on audience size and setting.

The Audio File

During Covid, when everything went online, I worked with sound artist Ben Addicott to create a sound file that sounded like being picked up in the present day and then dropped down into the future, compiled from recordings I made during the first lockdown. It works beautifully when you facilitate this online.[1]

The Magic Door

In smaller groups where we aren't constrained by fixed furniture, I invite participants to stand in a circle around me, provided the furniture can be moved out of the way and the room is big enough for people to stand in a circle. I ask them to close their eyes and imagine a door in front of them. A door that is made of wood, beautifully carved, and on the other side of which is 2030. It is a door that crackles with a kind of electricity. I then ask them in their own time to reach out, open that door, and to physically take a step through it. . .

The Hum

When doing this exercise in a large venue with fixed seats (like a theatre), I tell people that an important piece of this exercise is what a time machine sounds like. That without the sound to activate it, it won't work. I tell them that the sound is this (I start humming), 'but with you all joining in'. If the humming is a bit underwhelming, I tell them that there's no way we're going to be able to bend the space-time continuum with *that*, and we do it again until it's a bit louder. I ask them to close their eyes, we all hum together and off we go.

Travel to the Future

Whichever version we use, my instructions are then that we will sit in silence for a couple of minutes while they walk around that world of 2030. I tell them they need to use *all* of their senses. What does that world look like, smell like, taste like, feel like, sound like? You can also tailor the exercise to a particular context ('what does your school/business/city/campus look like?'). The room is silent. It's a magical experience standing watching a roomful of people doing it. You can hear a pin drop.

After a couple of minutes, I ask them, keeping their eyes closed, to turn to their neighbours (or if online, put them into paired breakout rooms) and spend a couple of minutes sharing with them what they saw/felt/heard/tasted/smelled. Keeping their eyes closed somehow helps to keep them in that space and makes the sharing richer and more vivid. I ask if anyone has impressions they'd like to share. In a large audience, having someone going around with a radio mic so everyone can hear those impressions really helps. In an online event, get people to use the chat to put in concise impressions and then read them out as they go past.

This time-machine exercise alone is a powerful one, something people often remember for years afterwards. In a workshop setting, there are a few things you could then follow it up with. The first is to capture what they experienced while time travelling in some tangible way. This could be:

Drawing. I give each group a large sheet of flipchart paper and some chunky pens or art materials and ask them to create a shared record of the future they imagined. It could be that they use images or, if no one feels competent as an artist, words. In one workshop I ran in Geneva, participants were given chalk pens and invited to draw on the windows. Some of them, rather smartly I thought, traced what they could see through the window and then adapted it for the future they had imagined.

Collage. If an organiser is able to source a big bunch of different magazines, some scissors and some glue, a lovely way to do this is by asking people to create collages of images. It also allows you to make the point that some magazines contain mostly adverts for cars and watches, and not so many images of how the future could be, and how important the media we consume is in terms of how possible we believe different futures to be.

Miro board. If you're facilitating this online you could use Miro or another platform that resembles a whiteboard with post-it notes on and ask people to note down their impressions.

Improvisation. You might ask them to devise and then act out scenarios from the future. A job interview? A parent/teacher meeting? An election hustings? Doing something creative and embodied can be a lot of fun.

Modelling. In the spirit of Town Anywhere, you might ask people to create models of what they imagined using cardboard, sticks, tape, pens. Use materials that give the maximum opportunity for the experience not to feel like school or work.

Writing. You might ask people to write some job adverts from the future, or a Tinder profile from a low-carbon future. Or perhaps the Classified Ads from the future? What are people looking for? What are they selling? Perhaps they are the newsreaders on the TV – which news stories might they be presenting?

'Making Scents of the Future'. This exercise is outlined in chapter 7 (see page 106).

Doing a combination of these can then lead into many different exercises, including Town Anywhere. After we've done this, I often tell people, before we stop for a break, 'Time travel is a powerful thing. You have just rearranged yourself at a quantum level, so you might feel a little discombobulated afterwards, it might take you a little while to feel fully present again, but it will settle. Research has shown that cake can act as a powerful grounding agent.'

The Walk of What If

If you have more time, and if you are working with an organisation that wants to go deeper in reimagining itself, you might follow up the time travelling with a Walk of What If. This activity follows on beautifully from time travelling. Having time travelled, it's important to find the ways to move visions and dreams into steps towards actual change in the world.

I always begin this by doing a version of the 'Yes, but. . . / Yes / Yes, and. . .' exercise, which I learned while studying improv. I begin by putting the group into pairs and tell them they are two friends planning a picnic together. In each pair, Person A suggests what they could bring for the picnic and Person B has to respond to their suggestion.

There are three rounds, and in the first round the person responding must agree to the suggestion but do so with as much negativity as they can ('Yes, but. . .'). In round two, the responder again agrees, this time in a less negative way but still with no enthusiasm at all ('Yes'). In the final round, Person B agrees and this time does so, full of excitement, and together the friends build an extraordinary and ridiculous story of what they will do together on their picnic ('Yes, and. . .'). Then sit back and watch as the room fills up with bright eyes, laughter and connection.

Here is an example of how this could go:

ROUND ONE (YES, BUT. . .)
Person A: 'I'll bring some sandwiches!'
Person B: 'Yes, but last time I ate your sandwiches I was in hospital for six months . . . Makes me feel sick thinking about it! Bleh!'

ROUND TWO (YES)
Person A: 'I'll make your favourite cake!'
Person B: 'Yes, well if you must. . .'

ROUND THREE (YES, AND. . .)
Person A: 'I'll bring champagne!'
Person B: 'Yes, and we could open a champagne bar down by the river!'
Person A: 'Yes, and we could invite Beyoncé to come and play the piano there!'
Person B: 'Yes and. . .', and so on.

The purpose of this activity is to demonstrate that these incredible and fantastical stories can only exist when we are listening to each other – by answering 'Yes, and. . .'.

The Walk of What If that follows has only two rules. The first is that, inspired by the 'Yes, but. . .' exercise they've just done, the words 'Yes, but' are banned. If someone makes a suggestion, you can only respond with a 'Yes, and'. The second rule is that you must not be constrained by what already exists. Don't think, 'But this isn't in our organisation's five-year development plan we just signed off.' Think bold and audacious and blue skies.

I put people into groups of five or six, and ask them to go for a walk. Go to the park, to the forest. I tell them to give their imaginations space. I suggest they set a timer on someone's phone so they can be back on time and you don't have to send out a search party to look for them. These conversations need to be framed by an overarching 'What If' question, which you have finely honed before so as to be most useful to them. For example, one we use quite a lot is, 'What if, in everything that it did, [insert name of organisation] acted as though this was a climate and ecological emergency?' But it can be tailored each time you do it.

I give groups a fistful of 'What If strips' (a sheet of A4 cut into 10 strips each with the words 'What If?' at one end) and tell them they need to be back in the room in an hour with as many 'What If' questions as they can come up with. I say that what we are looking for are the transformative 'What If' questions that people asked in the present day that unlocked the 2030 they dreamed of when they time travelled. Instruct them to keep them as actionable and grounded as possible. And off they go.

When they come back, brimming with questions, with fistfuls of 'What If' strips, exhilarated from the exploration, I tell them that one end of the room is 'really urgent' and the other end is 'not so urgent' and to imagine a line running from one to the other. I invite them, in conversation and negotiation with each other, to arrange their questions along this continuum.

Once this is done, we gather at the 'most urgent' end, and I read out the questions from that end, inviting people to step forward and offer to host a conversation on how that idea could be turned into a fully worked-up proposal, suggesting that anyone who would like to have that conversation goes and stands with them. Within a few minutes, groups have formed, and an hour later we hear back from the groups the implementable ideas they've come up with and thought through. The sight of hundreds of 'What If' strips laid out on the floor is one that I've come to love.

One last flourish that is nice to do is to gather up some of the strips at the end and stick them to sticky tape to make a curtain of strips. You then stick this across the door frame at head height to create a 'What If Carwash' that people have to pass through each time they enter or leave the room, brushing them with 'What If' goodness!

Sometimes, especially if you are working after the lunch break, you might need exercises up your sleeve to counteract droopy eyelids and the post-lunch energy slump. I'll give you one of my favourites, which I learned on an improv training I did. It's called 'Village Elders'. Form the group into circles of six to eight people. Everybody stands in a circle, shoulder to shoulder. They are told to imagine that they are all village elders with long earlobes, which are a sign of their wisdom and venerability.

They take it in turns to say a single word each, going round the circle. Their aim is to make a sentence, and when that sentence reaches a natural conclusion that sounds like it might be some philosophical phrase uttered by wise elders, everyone nods sagely and strokes their long earlobes and says 'Mmmmmmm'. Then they start again, and so on, until you feel it's time to draw it to a close. Sometimes I play this game where the idea is to formulate policies for the place where the course is taking place, as though they were local policymakers, but policymakers who use the same approach as the village elders. With this version, it can be good each time to have someone who writes them down and then at the end hear some of the policy ideas back.

What's beautiful about this is that it helps to put us into a headspace where there are no right answers, and there is no judgement about what people come up with. Sometimes a real gem emerges that no one would have expected that really takes everyone by surprise. (It does also run the danger that for weeks afterwards, if you're in a setting where someone says something you agree with, you start stroking your earlobes and going 'Mmmmmmmmm'. It's not unheard of.)

So, there you have it. You can now open a time portal wherever and whenever you choose. You can do it anywhere, and with anyone. Bring your 'unshakable certainty and deadpan humour', your sense of theatricality and playfulness, and see what happens.

What might these and other tools look like if they were scaled up – to the scale of a movement dedicated to the nurturing of longing? For me, one thing is clear. Any movement dedicated to the nurturing of longing will only be successful if it includes the people in our culture who are skilled at cultivating longing. Who are those people? Are they climate scientists? No. Are they climate activists? Generally not. They are poets, screenwriters, science-fiction writers, people who work in advertising, scriptwriters, street artists, novelists, musicians, perfumiers, designers, artists, chefs, dancers, set designers, filmmakers, rappers, people who are brilliant at projecting light onto buildings. There will be many others that I've forgotten, but you get the idea. We need them all, and we need to then co-create what this revolution of longing could actually look like.

In 2021, I was a speaker at an online conference organised by Ubisoft, one of the largest creators of video games in the world. I had to tell them at the beginning, in the spirit of full disclosure, that the last video game I played with any level of enthusiasm was *Pac-Man*, so perhaps I wasn't their guy. The question being explored was what role could video games play in spreading ideas about sustainability.

My contribution was that these stories need to become the background for the stories we tell, to become just a new normal to us. Video games like *Assassin's Creed* create entire immersive worlds, one of which, *Assassin's Creed Origins*, released in 2017, rendered the world of ancient Egypt incredibly accurately after a team of 1,000 developers with a budget of $125 million worked for years with historians, academics and researchers to build the most faithful representation of that ancient world yet created. It's so extraordinary that history teachers use it with their students.[2] And yet, I imagine, ask most players of that game to describe what a low-carbon, more just and equal future would look like, and they'd look at you, puzzled. Imagine the extraordinary low-carbon, more resilient, biodiverse and just future Ubisoft and countless other designers of films, video games and novels could have brought alive with those kinds of resources to play with. As I said, we need them all.

What if, one day, a call goes out for a day of 'Summoning the Future to the Capital', a huge mobilisation that invites people to surround Parliament with things that for them symbolise the future they most long for? It taps into a huge diversity of movements for change, as well as artists, writers, activists, actors, farmers, renewable energy installers and rewilders, each of whom bring a living, breathing, interactive vision of the future to the streets. Some bring a plant or some fruit they've grown, furniture they've made, musical instruments, toy beavers, their children. They take the time to share with each other what that object represents, the hope it embodies.

Perhaps young people, initially mobilised by Fridays for Future, bring moving representations of the future they long to see, the dreams they cling to and are determined to see realised. Afrofuturists bring art, story, music and a deep embodied sense of what a future rooted in Afrofuturism would look like. Actors perform short pieces that speak to the future of their longing, that transport people there. Food campaigners cook thousands of free meals for people.[3] Others bring trees and position them where a city with a better urban canopy would have trees. One group sets up a 2030 Employment Agency, highlighting the huge number of new jobs this future has created.[4] Teachers from across the country gather to celebrate the new curriculum of 2030, the ending of testing, the new era for creative education that has just begun. Copies of *A People's Encyclopedia 2070* are distributed and celebrated. Street artists create glimpses of the future on the walls of the present.

Activists from local authorities across the country meet to share their reimagining of local government. There is dedicated space for children's play. It is a safe and inclusive space for women, people of colour and LGBTQ+ people, just as this future will be. A huge, vibrant and dazzling time portal has been opened that allows many thousands of people to step in and experience it.

Every workshop that takes place begins with the words 'Here in 2030'. Tour guides take people on imaginary tours of nearby streets, conjuring up in their imaginations what it now feels like to walk through 2030. It is a day that is thrilling, that deeply touches people, that confounds the media with its brazenly positive vision of how the future could be, and the joy people experience on the streets. As a result, many thousands of people fall in love with the future, and the momentum to create it begins to build.

What else might such a mobilisation look like? That's rather up to you. Luigi Vitali offers a taste of it when he writes, 'Only a collective inclusive vision holds the power to reclaim the future. A vision able to contrast the present stagnation and paralysis of short-term thinking; one able to reject the illusion that nothing can change, that power will always prevail, that ideals are naïve.'[5]

It's almost time to put this book down and tell the people you love most about the future you long for. Maybe that means rivers so clean you could swim to work.[6] Or living in a natural world visibly regenerating itself. Paint for them seductive pictures of the world that we could still create, pictures rooted in our collective liberation, in deep democracy, in becoming good stewards of this extraordinary planet, of a more just and fairer world.

Point them to the stories of the pioneer projects in the present where these things are already working, where you can already see and touch and taste them. Share with them smells you've collected to help bring it alive. Play them some *Field Recordings from the Future*. Make your own. Create events, utopian moments, tastes of the futures we're told are 'impossible', that give other people the opportunity to undertake that adventure too. Design thrilling ways of summoning the future.

Perhaps we could adapt Victorian 'tell your future' end-of-the-pier machines to give people positive futures: 'Your street just planted thirty fruit trees in depaved areas, everyone helped and feels really proud.' Or, 'It's now five years since you started cycling to work along your city's excellent new cycle paths, and you feel so much fitter as a result.' That kind of thing.

If you're part of a movement, a campaign, an organisation, build the capacity, the skillset, within that organisation to become as good at talking about the future it wants to create as it is at talking about what's broken in the present. Many seem to be wondering what the next evolution of the activism needed to shift things might look like, in these days where time has nearly run out and tyrants rise to meet us at every turn. As Anthea Lawson, author of *The Entangled Activist*, recently wrote:

> *Am noticing there's lots of people that Extinction Rebellion woke up to taking action on climate who are currently marking time, looking for the next thing. A bit like where you hop about waving hands to the quieter bit of a tune, waiting for the beat to drop and everyone will LET RIP.*[7]

I would so love to see a civil society futurist movement rooted in the 'potential impossible [which] is calling softly and knocking gently', as Sun Ra puts it; a movement that extends beyond civil society and into local authorities, businesses, education and many other places. It's not a novel idea. T.J. Demos in *Radical Futurisms* writes that he 'finds in radical futurisms the promise of a widespread movement capable of world-historic action'.[8] Now that would be exhilarating.

Afterword

When I was eighteen, I read Angela Carter's extraordinary 1972 novel *The Infernal Desire Machines of Doctor Hoffman*. As my writing process draws to a close, and as the world takes shape through the second coming of President Donald Trump, Carter's book comes back into my imagination often. It tells the story of a diabolical genius named Dr Hoffman who has developed a weapon, a kind of ray gun, to attack an unnamed South American city. When fired, the machines unleash mass hallucinations, causing the dreams and desires of the population to take physical form. Everybody begins to turn mad in what Carter describes as the 'phantasmagoric redefinition' of the city.[1]

> *Cloud palaces erected themselves then silently toppled to reveal for a moment the familiar warehouse beneath them until they were replaced by some fresh audacity. A group of chanting pillars exploded in the middle of a mantra and lo! they were once again street lamps until, with night, they changed to silent flowers. Giant heads in the helmets of conquistadors sailed up like sad, pained kites over the giggling chimney pots. Hardly anything remained the same for more than one second and the city was no longer the conscious production of humanity; it had become the arbitrary realm of dream.*[2]

When I first immersed myself in the world painted by Carter, a world in which nothing was as it seemed, where monsters and ghosts appeared from nowhere, and distinguishing between reality and nightmare was impossible, it was hard to square it with the real world around me. It felt like somewhere that existed between the pages of the book and nowhere else. In this new world, I no longer feel like that.

As I complete writing this book, not long into the return of the Trump administration, the world feels very much as though Dr Hoffman, like Trump, has returned from exile, and now we find ourselves in the sights of his new and improved Desire Machine. Nothing seems real anymore. The title of Carter's book when first published in the US was *The War of Dreams*. Sound familiar?

It's a bewildering world in which our enemies are now our friends and our friends are our enemies; scientists and government officials in the US can't use the phrases 'climate change' and 'social justice' anymore, as if somehow the existential problems they describe will magically disappear if we just stop talking about them. It's a 1+1=3 world, where presidents turn into emperors, where 'alternative' facts are prioritised over actual facts, where Nazi salutes pop up in the middle of talks as if it's completely normal. It's bewildering and exhausting.

We're left casting about for the familiar, unable to cling to even the basic things we assumed we would always be able to take for granted as insane executive order after insane executive order flies past us. Which bathroom trans people get to use is now apparently of far greater importance than the collapse of the Atlantic Meridional Overturning Circulation.[3] Is it us going mad or the world around us? What can we cling onto as being real anymore?

Resistance to this is taking many forms, all essential. In Carter's novel, the protagonist, Desiderio, is sent on a secret mission to find Dr Hoffman and destroy his Desire Machines. I can't help wondering, though, how the book might have played out if, instead, he had decided to stay put and pull together the city's finest minds to build a Desire Machine of his own; one designed to benefit humanity and to connect people to positive visions of the future. The thought I want to leave you with, as we draw this book to a close, is that perhaps our job now is to out-engineer Dr Hoffman and find new ways to work together to create the most powerful Desire Machines the world has yet seen.

How can we, urgently and at scale, bring alive for people what a future built on care, compassion, equality, social justice and having rapidly reduced our carbon emissions would look like, smell like, taste like? And how can we tell stories of that future that help people create a new North Star in their lives? I've shared with you many inspirational examples of artists, activists, writers and motivated folks in big organisations who are doing just that.

I've mentioned Field Recordings from the Future, the ambient music project I've been developing with Mr Kit. By the time you read this, the live immersive time portal tour we're building will be a reality: part-installation, part-gig space, part-immersive temporal fluidity experience. We believe that, if humanity is to race towards a future we'd be proud to leave to the generations yet unborn, a critical mass of us need to experience something so profound, so genuinely mind-blowing and multisensory, that it rips apart the 'yes, but. . .' narratives that tell us there is no alternative to the current system – and sweeps open doorways to a new way of being. This is the level of ambition we're working at.

The nurturing of longing is not necessarily an approach or a skillset that comes naturally to those of us in the resistance. The people in our culture who are great at nurturing imagination tend not to be activists. Rather, they are street artists, poets, designers, people who write TV series, people who work in advertising, people who design wildly imaginative festivals such as Boomtown.[4] If we are to build Desire Machines more powerful than those that currently have us bewitched, bewildered and bedazzled, we need to encourage a coming together of artists (in the widest sense of the word) and activists on a scale we've never seen before. It is my dream that this book might play a role in inspiring and catalysing that coming together.

This could be through creating 'utopian moments' such as performers in public spaces acting out scenarios from the future that turned out OK – 'pop-up tomorrows' that touch people emotionally. Street art can also bring that future into the present. Artists like Sophie Mess, ATM and Mona Caron create vibrant, beautiful murals with huge images of birds, wild plants and insects Dr Hoffman would be proud of – images that give us a taste of a different future in the here and now.[5]

We're done with dystopias. We're awash with them. They paralyse us: we've had enough. Cast them from our cinemas and toss them from the bookshelves.

Fascists hate creativity, imagination, daring, playfulness and people who speak of dreams and build pictures of a future predicated on decency, compassion, courage and connection. Our ability to organise and resist is vital, but I also believe, now more than ever, that our true strength will lie in our ability to cultivate longing – to build awesome Desire Machines. I'm digging out my toolbox and heading to the garage to start building mine. Who's joining me?

Acknowledgements

To the people who have particularly supported me on the journey of creating this book: My family, my mighty editor Brianne Goodspeed, Susan Pegg, Rose Baldwin, Muna Reyal and the whole team at Chelsea Green, Ariane Conrad, everyone at Transition Network, Mr Kit, Transition activists everywhere, Nick Anim, Phoebe Tickell, Brian Eno, Filipa Pimentel, Penny A. Hay, Richard Couldrey, Yaz Brien, Chris McCartney, Cyril Dion for assuring me this book was a good idea, Frances Northrop, Carly and Ian Trisk-Grove, Joanna Smith, Jo Hook, Luke Mitchell and everyone at Boomtown, Tamzin Pinkerton, Guillaume Sanchez, Max Fawcett and all the crew, Stephane Gitton, Elke Helmi, Xavier Combe, Magali Chouvion, Julien Dezecot, Jon Alexander, Gillian Judson, Michael Datura, Rachel Breviere, Thomas Liera, everyone at Team Love, Peter Lipman, Rob Shorter, Jay Tompt, Coventry Refugee and Migrant Centre, Drum, Tim Dollimore, Jamyang Buddhist Centre London, Fred Mulder, Lucy Neal, Ben Brangwyn, Charles Blass, Julien Guimard, Amber Massie-Blomfield, everyone at L'Apres M in Marseille, Erika Zarate and Alba Danés Boix at Resilience.Earth

All the people I interviewed for this book: Dominic Acland, Donna Rose Addis, Shasta Hanif Ali, Astrid Hørby Aller, Jackie Andrade, Iris Andrews, Pierre-André Aubert, Anna Bailey, Ruth Ben Tovim, Justine Boussard, adrienne maree brown, Damien Careme, Andy Clee, John Corbett, Dan Edelstyn, Ed Finn, Justine Focone, Ben Goldfarb, Jo Grover, Paul Hawken, Hal Herschfield, Hsuan L. Hsu, Dr Nikitah

Okembe-RA Imani, Walidah Imarisha, Anab Jain, Indy Johar, Chris Jones, Mariame Kaba, Peter Kalmus, Roman Krznaric, Ouassima Laabich, Marai Larasi, Sam Lee, Anne Lehelloco, Helen Lucocq, Marina McDougall, Bridget McKenzie, Florian Malzacher, Jon May, Brian Meeks, Gemma Mortensen, Frances Northrop, Jo Orchard-Webb, Soodàbè Oulàdi, Lauren Parater, Kirsty Rose Parker, Gilles Perole, Rachel Phillips, Annaïg Plassard, Hilary Powell, Lorna Prescott, Jacob Rask, Jonathan Rhodes, Ella Saltmarshe, Manda Scott, Promona Sengupta, Aisha Shillingford, William Sites, Cauleen Smith, Tibet Sprague, Jonas Staal, Rashni Stanford, Thomas Stanley, Karl Szpunar, Gabriel Teodros, Phoebe Tickell, Camille Turner, Mama D Ujuaje, Hanna Thomas Uose, Jeanne van Heeswijk and Mushon Zer-Aviv. Thank you all so much for your time.

To everyone who supported me on Patreon (patreon.com/fromwhatiftowhatnext) during the writing of this book. I couldn't have done this without you: Isobel Bros, Cécile Vava, Rema Teller, Steve Creffield, Thyr Björnson, Joanna White, Keri Jarvis, Barbara Smith, Georgeann Johnson, Boris Krieglstein, Dave Dave, Mélissa Buecher-Nelson, Helen Lucocq, Eva Svenstedt Ward, Mal Williams, Kris Morton, Larry Edwards, Mona Zeutschel, Annette Hennessy, Kati Saqui, Simon Ruston, Rina Jones, Tina Leonard, Christopher Cooke, Mike Adams, Grit Belitz, Michelle, Thierry Hoyois, Paul Quinn, Dave Harvey, Robert, Laura, Gary Pace, Birte Peters, Florencia, Alexander McConnell, Caitlin Keeley, Marlene Rathgeber, Sami Starling, Isabel Shaida, Tamzin Pinkerton, LaUra Schmidt, Deb Joffe, Andrea Gilly, Raphaela L, Sean, Joel Rogers, Annie Heck, Tanya Steinhauser, Ian H McGregor, Ruth Shaber, Jon McLeod, Jesper Cockx, kaeko, Lorraine Jones, Gemma Mallol, Sophy, Andy Lyon, Ross Walker, Laura-Jane Smith, Oskar Stokholm Østergaard, Nicole Strong, Ali Gordon-Creed, Andrew Kennard, Becky

Gale, Don Hall, Debs Erwin, Christine Hopkins, Maria Gee, Evrard Broquet, Daniel Mohr, Samantha Drury Shore, David Somervell, Andrew Langford, Marcus Bussey, Michael Hubicki, Kate Campbell, Rosie Pearson, John Cooper, Felix Scholtes, Steff Wright, Jonathan Meth, Julia Lim, Ines Heinrich, Ed Bailey, Lisa Mason, Annabel Cameron-Duff, Aliyah Norrish, Rhona Clews, Anne-Marie Fuller, Kate Parkins, Muriel Stallworth, Terri Kaye, Barbara Bingham, Neil Bee, Eva Moldovanyi, Jane Baker, Mary Mowbray, Jen Wright, Eva-Maria McCormack, John Booth, Anna Fox, Beth Barany, Heather Jones, Felix, Catherine Johnstone, Penny Baird, Kirsty Logan, Alan Wiseman, Stewart Clements, Tore S Kristiansen, Grant Abert, Jules Maitland, Dan Shipsides, Mary Light, Dan Lockton, Axel Schmidt, Mary Stevens, Colby Williams, Leslie Smith, Rita J. King, Flora Collingwood-Norris, Sabrina, Rebecca Phelan, Stefanie Rueckert, Kathleen Quinn, David Takahashi, Barry Cohen, John Marshall, Sandra Duggan, John Allen, Becky Lythgoe, Paul McHugh, John A Duvall, Joanna Machowska, Meg Walker, Richard Bell, Mark G Lonsdale, Peter Jones, Paul Leech, Eileen Wylicil, Dora Napolitano, Markus Zeindlinger, Charlotte Lloyd Webber, Cassie Robinson, Robert McFaul, Clare Diaper, Gabriela Endele, Joy Marie Lee Iglesias, Becky Thatcher, Nava Israel, Jane Gallagher, Mark Baverstock, Kevin Lindsay, Céline Delhaye, Kathryn Pratt, Charlie Pratt, Brian Fernandes-Halloran, Emi Slater, Laura Lumsden, Davo Ruthven-Stuart, Laura Singleton, Marc Grandgirard, Liz Ware, Nathaniel Stott, Roisin Markham, John Reed, Barbara A Jones, Jonathan Lill, Benjamin Taylor, Paul Galles, Luis Adamson, Delphine Scholl, Mary Pattison, Sabine Reitmaier, Andreia Carvalho, Morey Bean, Sarah Fraser, Sarah Colwell, Emma Leaf-Grimshaw, Jo Bolton, Erica Naylor, Pritam Singh, Eimear McNally, Jimmy Buff, Jonathan Smith, Beth Barlow, Sheena, Anne White, David Ashton, Zoe Davis, Douglas Bonar, Trisha Comrie, Tobias Adriansson,

Liz Batten, Johny Diderich, Imogen Storey, Sarah McAdam, Ruth Doherty, Elke Himmelmann, Norry Schneider, Rosie Cooper, Alan Smith, Gemma Mortensen, Ken Huggins, Eric Jong, Aniela Fidler Wieruszewska, Pierre Clause, Andrew Mackay, Richard Couldrey, David Cutting, Sarah Speakman-Jones, Lin Patterson, Freya Hardy, Karin Eyben, Romany Buck, Lorenzo Ci, Tony Buck, Adam Whitworth, Lindum Greene, Johoney, Clare Jackson, Eleanor Gwendoline Hale, Wilf Macdonald-Brown, appleturnover, John Ingleby, Chris Wells, Claire Garrett, Patricia Lee, Pamela Barnes, Scott McAulay, Sarah Hodgkiss, Erica Lewis, Mike Grenville, Keith, Looby Macnamara.

Those who have fired my own imagination during the writing of this book: Sun Ra, Vincent Van Gogh, John Coltrane, Saidiya Hartman, Geir Aule Jenssen, Ryan Griffin, Rasheedah Phillips, Camae Ayewa, Robin D.G. Kelley, Alex Zamalin, Jayna Brown, Tirzah Garwood, Eric Ravilious, Gisèle Pelicot, Angela Davis, Robyn Maynard, Alice Coltrane, Sheila Robinson, John Nash, Edward Bawden, Leanne Betasamosake Simpson, Dr Jan Willis, Max Haiven, Mary Lattimore, Jon Hopkins, Rebecca Solnit, Caroline (the band), Carlo Rovelli, Transitioners everywhere, Chloe Naldrett, Annalee Newitz, Charles Yu, Lauren MacDonald, Boards of Canada, Andrew PM Hunt (Dialect), Idles, and everyone who continues to dream big and speak truth to power in these most dangerous of days.

Recommended Resources

Books

Abdullah, Ahmed. *A Strange Celestial Road: My Time in the Sun Ra Arkestra*. Blank Forms Editions, 2023.

Adam, Barbara. *Time*. Polity Press, 2004.

Benjamin, Ruha. *Imagination: A Manifesto*. W.W. Norton & Company, 2024.

Boulding, Elise. *Into Full Flower: Making Peace Cultures Happen*. Dialogue Path Press, 2010.

Bradley, Kaliane. *The Ministry of Time*. Sceptre, 2024.

Bregman, Rutger. *Utopia for Realists: How We Can Build the Ideal World*. Little, Brown, 2017.

brown, adrienne maree and Walidah Imarisha. *Octavia's Brood: Science Fiction Stories from Social Justice Movements*. AK Press, 2015.

brown, adrienne maree. *Emergent Strategy: Shaping Change, Changing Worlds*. AK Press, 2017.

Brown, Jayna. *Black Utopias: Speculative Life and the Music of Other Worlds*. Duke University Press, 2021.

Brunner, Bernd. *Moon: A Brief History*. Yale University Press, 2010.

Butler, Octavia E. *Kindred*. Headline, 2014.

Clegg, Brian. *Build Your Own Time Machine: The Real Science of Time Travel*. Duckworth Overlook, 2013.

Davidson, Jane. *#futuregen: Lessons from a Small Country*. Chelsea Green Publishing, 2020.

Demos, T.J. *Radical Futurisms: Ecologies of Collapse, Chronopolitics, and Justice-to-Come*. Sternberg Press, 2023.

Eshun, Ekow. *In the Black Fantastic*. MIT Press, 2022.

Gleick, James. *Time Travel: A History*. Pantheon Books, 2016.

Goldfarb, Ben. *Eager: The Surprising, Secret Life of Beavers and Why They Matter*. Chelsea Green Publishing, 2019.

Gow, Derek. *Bringing Back the Beaver: The Story of One Man's Quest to Rewild Britain's Waterways*. Chelsea Green Publishing, 2020.

Griffiths, Jay. *Pip Pip: A Sideways Look at Time*. Flamingo, 1999.

Gunkel, Henriette and kara lynch, eds. *We Travel the Space Ways: Black Imagination, Fragments, and Diffractions*. Transcript, 2019.

Haskell, David George. *Sounds Wild and Broken: Sonic Marvels, Evolution's Creativity and the Crisis of Sensory Extinction*. Faber, 2022.

Hemphill, Prentis. *What It Takes to Heal: How Transforming Ourselves Can Change the World*. Random House, 2024.

Hsu, Hsuan L. *The Smell of Risk: Environmental Disparities and Olfactory Aesthetics*. NYU Press, 2020.

Kelley, Robin D.G. *Freedom Dreams: The Black Radical Imagination*. Beacon Press, 2002.

Krznaric, Roman. *History for Tomorrow: Inspiration from the Past for the Future of Humanity*. Penguin Books, 2024.

Lawson, Anthea. *The Entangled Activist: Learning to Recognise the Master's Tools*. Perspectiva, 2021.

MacDonald, Benedict. *Cornerstones: Wild Forces That Can Change Our World*. Bloomsbury, 2022.

McGonigal, Jane. *Imaginable: How to See the Future Coming and Be Ready for Anything*. Bantam Press, 2022.

Monbiot, George. *Feral: Rewilding the Land, Sea and Human Life*. Penguin Books, 2014.

Muñoz, José Esteban. *Cruising Utopia: The Then and There of Queer Futurity*. New York University Press, 2009.

Murphy, Ben. *Ears To The Ground: Adventures in Field Recording and Electronic Music*. Velocity Press, 2024.

Nanni, Giordano. *The Colonisation of Time: Ritual, Routine and Resistance in the British Empire*. Manchester University Press, 2012.

Newitz, Annalee. *The Future of Another Timeline*. Little Brown, 2019.

Phillips, Rasheedah. *Dismantling the Master's Clock: On Race, Space, and Time*. AK Press, 2025.

Rifkin, Jeremy. *Time Wars: The Primary Conflict in Human History*. Touchstone Books, 1989.

Rovelli, Carlo. *The Order of Time*. Penguin Books, 2019.

Scott, Manda. *Any Human Power*. September Publishing, 2024.

Sites, William. *Sun Ra's Chicago: Afrofuturism and the City*. University of Chicago Press, 2020.

Szwed, John F. *Space is the Place: The Lives and Times of Sun Ra*. Mojo Books, 2000.

Toop, David. *Ocean of Sound: Ambient Sound and Radical Listening in the Age of Communication*. Serpent's Tale Publishing, 1997.

Tullett, William. *Smell and the Past: Noses, Archives, Narratives*. Bloomsbury Publishing, 2023.

Wallace-Wells, David. *The Uninhabitable Earth: A Story of the Future*. Penguin Books, 2019.

Womack, Ytasha L. *Afrofuturism: The World of Black Sci-Fi and Fantasy Culture*. Lawrence Hill Publishing, 2013.

Zamalin, Alex. *Black Utopia: The History of an Idea from Black Nationalism to Afrofuturism*. Columbia University Press, 2019.

Websites

Atmos Totnes: www.totnescommunity.org.uk.
Black Quantum Futurism: www.blackquantumfuturism.com.
Intra-Galactic Forest: https://streetworkproject.net/intra-galactic-forest.
Justine Boussard: www.justineboussard.co.uk.
Le Présage: https://lepresage.fr/wp.
Moral Imaginations: www.moralimaginations.com.
New Constellations: https://newconstellations.co.
Peter Kalmus: https://peterkalmus.net.
Rob Hopkins: www.robhopkins.net.
Speculative Tourism: www.speculativetourism.com.
Woodland Valley Farm: https://woodlandvalley.co.uk/beavers.

Notes

Introduction

1. This book will often make references to 2030 as being the site of the future it dreams about. At the time of writing, that's not very far away, and by the time you pick this up, it'll be even less so. The temptation, therefore, would be to push it further out, to talk about 2035, 2040, 2050, to somehow be more 'pragmatic'. The reason I focus on that date is because the Paris Agreement, adopted in 2015, imperfect and inadequate as it is, still represents the best chance we have of a binding international response to climate change; it sets a target of cutting emissions 43 per cent by 2030 while firmly en route to zero by 2050. This is a book that explores what the 2030 that has achieved this may be like. This is not a book that will attempt to negotiate with physics. That has to remain the target. The reality is that we need to move, and we need to move fast, and to have any chance of avoiding spectacular climate collapse, the scale and urgency of what we need to do is real and non-negotiable. While it might be more palatable, more comfortable, to push it further away, a deadline is a deadline. This book, therefore, dares to ask: what could that 2030 be like if it were the result of our doing everything we could possibly have done? So, 2030 it is. If you're reading this in 2030, you'll know if we did the work or not.
2. Musician Sam Lee holds an event in woodlands in southern England, called Singing with Nightingales, on multiple dates between mid-April and the end of May. See: Singing with Nightingales, https://www.singingwithnightingales.co.uk.
3. Ruha Benjamin, *Imagination: A Manifesto* (W.W. Norton & Company, 2024), 8.
4. The Marshall Plan, named after the then US Secretary of State George C. Marshall, was the vehicle through which the US invested $13 billion into rebuilding Europe following World War II. Its focus was on stimulating a resurgence of European industry, keeping communist expansion at bay, and establishing a large market for American goods and services.
5. Katherine Rose quoted in Chris Baraniuk, 'The Cities Stripping Out Concrete for Earth and Plants', BBC Future, 23 February 2024, https://www.bbc.com/future/article/20240222-depaving-the-cities-replacing-concrete-with-earth-and-plants.

6. Portland, Oregon, is one city, among many, that has an active depaving movement. See: Depave, https://www.depave.org.
7. Kathryn Gilstad-Hayden et al., 'Research Note: Greater Tree Canopy Cover Is Associated with Lower Rates of Both Violent and Property Crime in New Haven, CT', *Landscape and Urban Planning* 143 (2015): 248–253, https://doi.org/10.1016/j.landurbplan.2015.08.005.
8. The City of Hamburg has established a target of 70 per cent of suitable roofs to be turned into gardens, with an allocation of €3 million to encourage the adoption of green roofs across the city, both on new and renovated buildings. See: 'Green Roofs', Hamburg, 28 August 2017, https://www.hamburg.com/residents/green/green-roofs-19000.
9. Sponge cities, a concept that originated in China, has been adopted in Shanghai, New York and Cardiff, where stakeholders are implementing a range of strategies to increase their porosity and water storage with nature-based solutions. See: Leah Hudson Leva, 'Urbanism 101: What is a Sponge City?', The Urbanist, 8 February 2023, https://www.theurbanist.org/2023/02/08/urbanism-101-what-is-a-sponge-city.
10. At least as far back as 2002, environmentalists and land protectors around the world were being killed because of their activism. In 2014, Global Witness published its landmark report that verified 908 such activists had been killed between 2002 and 2013. Since then, it has published annual reports that names those killed while defending their land and environment during the previous year. Its most recent report named 196 activists murdered in 2023 alone. See: 'Land and Environmental Defenders: Annual Report Archive', Global Witness, 26 March 2020, https://www.globalwitness.org/en/campaigns/environmental-activists/land-and-environmental-defenders-annual-report-archive.
11. Aaron Regunberg and Donald Braman, 'A Big Tool to Fight Climate Change Is Hiding in Plain Sight', *New Republic*, 21 May 2024, https://newrepublic.com/article/181721/fossil-fuels-civil-forefeiture-pipeline-climate.
12. Another legal tool could be the Climate Superfund Act, which holds oil companies financially responsible for climate damages. It started in Vermont in 2024 and was rapidly replicated across the world. It enables states, and elsewhere nations, to assess the total costs to that state from greenhouse gas emissions back to a date at which it considers that a company was aware of the results of its actions. It began in Vermont because the previous year floods had caused $1 billion in damages. See: Dharna Noor, '"Game-Changing": Vermont Becomes First State to Require Big Oil to Pay for Climate Damages', *Guardian*, 31 May 2024, https://www.theguardian.com/us-news/article/2024/may/31/vermont-oil-companies-climate-superfund-act.
13. See: Climate Reframe, https://climatereframe.co.uk.

14. You will find all the episodes of *From What If to What Next* everywhere you get your podcasts.

Chapter 1: The Situation Is Urgent

1. Damian Carrington, 'We Asked 380 Top Climate Scientists What They Felt About the Future… They Are Terrified, but Determined to Keep Fighting. Here's What They Said', *Guardian*, 8 May 2024, https://www.theguardian.com/environment/ng-interactive/2024/may/08/hopeless-and-broken-why-the-worlds-top-climate-scientists-are-in-despair.
2. United Nations Environment Programme, *Emissions Gap Report 2022: The Closing Window – Climate Crisis Calls for Rapid Transformation of Societies* (Nairobi: United Nations Environment Programme, 2022), xxii, https://www.unep.org/resources/emissions-gap-report-2022.
3. Our World in Data, 'Per Capita Consumption-Based CO_2 Emissions', Global Carbon Project, 21 November 2024, https://ourworldindata.org/grapher/consumption-co2-per-capita; Oxfam, 'Carbon Emissions of Richest 1% Set to Be 30 Times the 1.5°C Limit in 2030', press release, 5 November 2021, https://www.oxfam.org/en/press-releases/carbon-emissions-richest-1-set-be-30-times-15degc-limit-2030; Institute for Global Environmental Strategies, Aalto University and D-mat ltd, *1.5-Degree Lifestyles: Targets and Options for Reducing Lifestyle Carbon Footprints. Technical Report* (Institute for Global Environmental Strategies, 2019).
4. Paul Hawken, *Regeneration: Ending the Climate Crisis in One Generation* (Penguin Random House, 2021), 253.
5. Bernice Harrison, 'The LA Climate Scientist Who Foresaw His Neighbourhood's Destruction and Left', *Irish Times*, 17 January 2025, https://www.irishtimes.com/podcasts/in-the-news/why-this-climate-scientist-moved-from-la-two-years-ago-and-why-he-says-nowhere-is-safe.
6. Vimal Patel, 'Climate Activists, Including Scientists, are Arrested in Protests at Private Airports', *New York Times*, 10 November 2022, https://www.nytimes.com/2022/11/10/us/private-jets-climate-protests-airport.html.
7. Cathy Rogers, Marcus Ostarek, Mabli Jones and James Özden, *What Was the Impact of the Insulate Britain Campaign?* (Social Change Lab, 2024), https://2ed91cf7-c25d-453e-a3d5-a90f73ccb6ab.usrfiles.com/ugd/2ed91c_4112e779eaf240ebb3f119082f423b40.pdf.
8. Elena Berton, 'Flight Shaming Hits Air Travel as "Greta Effect" Takes Off', Reuters, 2 October 2019, https://www.reuters.com/article/world/flight-shaming-hits-air-travel-as-greta-effect-takes-off-idUSKBN1WH23F.

9. Somini Sengupta, 'Young Women Are Leading Climate Protests. Guess Who Runs Global Talks?', *New York Times*, 6 November 2021, https://www.nytimes.com/2021/11/06/climate/climate-activists-glasgow-summit.html.
10. Caroline Douhaire, 'The Climate Decision of the German Constitutional Court and Its Implications on Soil Management', in *International Yearbook of Soil Law and Policy 2022*, eds. Harald Ginzky et al. (Springer, Cham, 2024), 35–50, https://doi.org/10.1007/978-3-031-40609-6_2.
11. Adrienne Buller, 'Major Banks are Abandoning Their Climate Alliance en Masse. So Much for "Woke Capital"', *Guardian*, 15 January 2025, https://www.theguardian.com/commentisfree/2025/jan/15/woke-capital-net-zero-banking-alliance.
12. HeeKyoung Chun et al., 'Maternal Exposure to Air Pollution and Risk of Autism in Children: A Systematic Review and Meta-Analysis', *Environmental Pollution* 256 (2020): 113307, https://doi.org/10.1016/j.envpol.2019.113307.
13. Andre Rhoden-Paul, 'Boat Race: Oxford Rowers Criticise Sewage Levels in River Thames', BBC News, 31 March 2024, https://www.bbc.com/news/uk-68701486.
14. Carlos Corvalan et al., 'Mental Health and the Global Climate Crisis', *Epidemiology and Psychiatric Sciences* 31, no. e86 (2022): 1–10, https://doi.org/10.1017/S2045796022000361.
15. Erika Karp and Derek Yach, *A Crisis of Our Time: Exploring the Global Rise of Mental Illness Through Economics, Lived Experiences, and Expert Insights* (Aspen Institute, 2024), https://www.aspeninstitute.org/wp-content/uploads/2024/07/FLF-Crisis-Report-392.pdf.
16. World Health Organization, *World Mental Health Report: Transforming Mental Health for All* (World Health Organization, 2022), https://www.who.int/teams/mental-health-and-substance-use/world-mental-health-report.
17. Oxfam International, 'Richest 1% Bag Nearly Twice as Much Wealth as the Rest of the World Put Together over the Past Two Years', press release, 16 January 2023, https://www.oxfam.org/en/press-releases/richest-1-bag-nearly-twice-much-wealth-rest-world-put-together-over-past-two-years.
18. Oxfam, 'Top 5 Ways Billionaires are Driving Climate Change', press release, 20 November 2023, https://www.oxfamamerica.org/explore/stories/top-5-ways-billionaires-are-driving-climate-change.
19. See: Transition Network, https://transitionnetwork.org.
20. Christiana Figueres, Tom Rivett-Carnac and Paul Dickinson, hosts, Outrage and Optimism, episode 241, 40 Seconds to Save the World, Paul Goodenough, 18 April 2024, 24:26, https://www.outrageandoptimism.org/episodes/40-seconds-to-save-the-world-with-paul-goodenough.

21. Daniel Steinmetz-Jenkins, 'Wendy Brown: A Conversation on Our "Nihilistic" Age', *The Nation*, 10 January 2024, https://www.thenation.com/article/culture/wendy-brown-interview.
22. Luigi Vitali, 'Editor's Letter: Uncancelling the Future', *Dust*, Winter/Spring 2025, 26–7.
23. You will find many excellent examples of this in Jane McGonigal, *Imaginable: How to See the Future Coming and Be Ready for Anything* (Bantam Press, 2022).
24. Susan Griffin, 'To Love the Marigold', in *The Impossible Will Take a Little While: Perseverance and Hope in Troubled Times*, ed. Paul Rogat (Basic Books, 2014), 171.

Chapter 2: Time Is More Fluid Than We Think

1. As far as I can tell, the T-shirt was the work of an organisation called Rebel Threads that no longer exists, and most image searches online now just bring up photos of ways in which I have subsequently used it. But honouring the origin of things is important.
2. 'Climate Stripes', University of Reading, 17 June 2021, https://www.reading.ac.uk/planet/climate-resources/climate-stripes.
3. Elise Boulding, 'A Journey into the Future: Imagining a Nonviolent World', *Peace and Conflict Studies* 9, no. 1 (2002): 52, http://dx.doi.org/10.46743/1082-7307/2002.1023.
4. Boulding, 'A Journey into the Future', 52.
5. Elise Boulding, 'The Challenge of Imaging Peace in Wartime', *Futures* 23, no. 5 (1991): 528–33, https://doi.org/10.1016/0016-3287(91)90100-G.
6. Piotr M. Szpunar and Karl K. Szpunar, 'Collective Future Thought: Concept, Function, and Implications for Collective Memory Studies', *Memory Studies* 9, no. 4 (2016): 376–389; Meymune N. Topcu and William Hirst, 'Collective Mental Time Travel: Current Research and Future Directions', *Progress in Brain Research* 274, no. 1 (2022): 71-97, https://doi.org/10.1016/bs.pbr.2022.06.002.
7. Shayla Love, 'Collective Mental Time Travel Can Influence the Future', *Wired*, 9 November 2022, https://www.wired.com/story/psychology-mental-time-travel-politics.
8. Susan Gaidos, 'Thanks for the Future Memories: To the Brain, Remembering the Past and Visualizing the Future Look Surprisingly Similar', *Science News* 173, no. 19 (2008): 26-29.
9. Laura Marsh et al., 'Positivity Bias in Past and Future Episodic Thinking: Relationship with Anxiety, Depression, and Retrieval Induced Forgetting', *Quarterly Journal of Experimental Psychology* 72, no. 3 (2018): 508–522.

10. Caitlin Mills and Kalina Christoff, 'Constructed Futures' in *Memory*, eds. Philippe Tortell, Mark Turin and Margot Young (UCB Press, 2018).
11. Marsh et al., 'Positivity Bias in Past and Future Episodic Thinking', 508–22.
12. Daniel T. Gilbert and Timothy D. Wilson, 'Prospection: Experiencing the Future', *Science* 317 (2007): 1351–54.
13. Gary P. Brown at al., 'Worry and the Simulating Future Outcomes', *Anxiety, Stress and Coping: An International Journal* 15, no. 1 (2002): 1–17.
14. Roland G. Benoit, Karl K. Szpunar and Daniel L. Schacter, 'Ventromedial Prefrontal Cortex Supports Affective Future Simulation by Integrating Distributed Knowledge', *PNAS* 111, no.46 (2014): 16550–555.
15. Shelley E. Taylor et al., 'Harnessing the Imagination: Mental Simulation, Self-Regulation and Coping', *American Psychologist* 53, no. 4 (1998): 429-30.
16. Julian W. Fernando et al., 'Functions of Utopia: How Utopian Thinking Motivates Societal Engagement', *Personality and Social Psychology Bulletin* 44 (2018): 779–92.
17. Julian W. Fernando et al., 'Greens or Space Invaders: Prominent Utopian Themes and Effects on Social Change Motivation', *European Journal of Social Psychology* 50 (2020): 278–91.
18. David Hallford and Arnaud D'Argembeau, 'Why We Imagine Our Future: Introducing the Functions of Future Thinking Scale (FoFTS)', *Journal of Psychopathology and Behavioural Assessment* 44 (2022): 376–95.
19. David Ingvar, '"Memory of the Future": An Essay on the Temporal Organization of Conscious Awareness', *Human Neurobiology* 4, no. 3 (1985): 127–36.
20. Benoit et al., 'Ventromedial Prefrontal Cortex Supports Affective Future Simulation', 16550–555.
21. Prentis Hemphill, *What It Takes To Heal: How Transforming Ourselves Can Change the World* (Random House, 2024), 19.
22. See, for example: Joanna Macy and Chris Johnstone, *Active Hope: How to Face the Mess We're in with Unexpected Resilience and Creative Power* (New World Library, 2022); LaUra Schmidt, Aimee Lewis Reau and Chelsie Rivera, *How to Live in a Chaotic Climate: 10 Steps to Reconnect with Ourselves, Our Communities, and Our Planet* (Shambhala Publications, 2023); and the work of Sophy Banks and her Healthy Human Culture model: https://www.healthyhumanculture.com.
23. Wendy M. Johnson and Graham C.L. Davey, 'The Psychological Impact of Negative TV News Bulletins and the Catastrophising of Personal Worries', *British Journal of Psychology* 88 (1997): 85–91.
24. John Whaite, 'Baking Control of my Mental Health', Sustain, 15 May 2023, https://www.sustainweb.org/realbread/articles/may23-john-whaite-baking-control-mental-health.

25. Rob Hopkins, 'Rob Hopkins Speech Boomtown 2024 – Boomtown Goes Deeper', posted by Boomtown Festival, YouTube, 11:56, https://youtu.be/d959h4Be8lQ?si=0bBpJa8fKLYdGHOy.
26. TomakaTom, 'My Big Boomtown Revelation', Reddit, 14 August 2024, https://www.reddit.com/r/BoomtownFestival/comments/1esacpd/my_big_boomtown_revelation.

Chapter 3: The Superfuel That Gets Us There

1. Lewis Carroll, *Alice's Adventures in Wonderland* (Macmillan and Co., 1866), 8–9.
2. bell hooks, *All About Love: New Visions* (Harper Collins Publishers, 2001), 14.
3. Ruha Benjamin, *Imagination: A Manifesto* (W.W. Norton & Company, 2024), 8.
4. Bernt Brunner, *Moon: A Brief History* (Yale University Press, 2010) 120.
5. Michael Benson, 'Science Fiction Sent Man to the Moon', *New York Times*, 20 July 2019, https://www.nytimes.com/2019/07/20/opinion/sunday/moon-rockets-space-fiction.html.
6. 'Who is Houston?', National Air and Space Museum, 21 September 2022, https://airandspace.si.edu/stories/editorial/who-houston.
7. Michael Benson, 'Science Fiction Sent Man to the Moon', *New York Times*, 20 July 2019, https://www.nytimes.com/2019/07/20/opinion/sunday/moon-rockets-space-fiction.html.
8. Hanna Thomas Uose, 'The Most Creative Look To The Future: Imagination and Creative Practice in Service of Organizational Transformation', UN Global Pulse, 13 December 2023, https://www.unglobalpulse.org/document/the-most-creative-look-to-the-future-imagination-and-creative-practice-in-service-of-organizational-transformation. See also: Caroline Bassett, Ed Steinmueller and George Voss, 'Better Made Up: The Mutual Influence of Science fiction and Innovation', Nesta Working Paper No. 13/07, March 2013, https://media.nesta.org.uk/documents/better_made_up_the_mutual_influence_of_science_fiction_and_innovation.pdf.
9. Grant Faulkner, 'The Literature of Longing: Our longings Are Beyond Us, Yet They Take Root Deep in Our Being', Medium, 16 April 2023, https://grantfaulkner.medium.com/the-literature-of-longing-c1e0aa9f3de7.
10. Robert H. Lustig, *The Hacking of the American Mind: The Science Behind the Corporate Takeover of our Bodies and Brains* (Avery, 2019). See also: Dr Anna Lembke, *Dopamine Nation: Why Our Addiction to Pleasure is Causing Us Pain* (Headline, 2023).
11. Prentis Hemphill, *What It Takes to Heal: How Transforming Ourselves Can Change the World* (Random House, 2024), 15.
12. Faulkner, 'The Literature of Longing.'

13. James Gleick, *Time Travel: A History* (Pantheon Books, 2016), 24, 35.
14. Gleick, *Time Travel*, 47.
15. Gleick, *Time Travel,* 58.
16. Allen Everett and Thomas Roman, *Time Travel and Warp Drives: A Scientific Guide to Shortcuts Through Time and Space* (University of Chicago Press, 2012), 223.
17. Gleick, *Time Travel*, 57.
18. Mark Kaufman, 'Stephen Hawking Hosted a Party for Time Travelers, but No One Came', Mashable, 14 March 2018, https://mashable.com/article/stephen-hawking-time-travel-party.
19. Gleick, *Time Travel*, 51.
20. Gleick, *Time Travel*, 5.
21. Patrick Reinsborough, 'Giant Whispers: Narrative Power, Radical Imagination and a Future Worth Fighting For…', *Affinities: A Journal of Radical Theory, Culture, and Action* 4 , no. 2 (2010): 67.
22. Charles Yu, *How to Live Safely in a Science Fictionalal Universe* (Vintage, 2010) 164–5.
23. Ann VanderMeer and Jeff VanderMeer, 'Preface', in *The Time Traveller's Almanac: The Ultimate Treasury of Time Travel Short Stories*, eds. Ann VanderMeer and Jeff VanderMeer (Head of Zeus Ltd, 2013), ix.
24. Don DeLillo, *Underworld* (Picador, 1999), 11.

Chapter 4: Adjust Your Disbelief Suspenders

1. Jason Hickel and Dylan Sullivan, 'How Much Growth Is Required to Achieve Good Lives for All? Insights from Needs-Based Analysis', *World Development Perspectives* 35 (2024): 100612, https://doi.org/10.1016/j.wdp.2024.100612.
2. Alastair McIntosh, *Soil and Soul: People Versus Corporate Power* (Aurum Press, 2002), 139.
3. Patrick Reinsborough, 'Giant Whispers: Narrative Power, Radical Imagination and a Future Worth Fighting For…', *Affinities: A Journal of Radical Theory, Culture, and Action* 4, no. 2 (2010): 69, https://ojs.library.queensu.ca/index.php/affinities/article/view/6140.
4. Andrea Lulovicova and Stephane Bouissou, 'Assessment of Local Food Policies through a Territorial Life Cycle Approach', Sustainability 2023, 15(6), 474 (2023).
5. Lulovicova and Bouissou, 'Assessment of Local Food Policies', 474.
6. The Energy Saving Trust define Passivhaus as: 'buildings created to rigorous energy efficient design standards so that they maintain an almost constant temperature. Passivhaus buildings are so well constructed, insulated and ventilated that they retain heat from the sun and the activities of their occupants,

requiring very little additional heating or cooling.' See: 'What is Passivhaus? The Gold Standard in Energy Efficiency', Energy Saving Trust, updated 25 July 2022, https://energysavingtrust.org.uk/passivhaus-what-you-need-know.

7. Kat Barber, 'Freiburg: Germany's Futuristic City Set in a Forest', BBC News, 16 July 2022, https://www.bbc.com/travel/article/20200715-freiburg-germanys-futuristic-city-set-in-a-forest; 'Road Transport: Car Dominance Unbroken', Statistisches Bundesamt, updated 21 February 2025, https://www.destatis.de/Europa/EN/Topic/Transport/Car.html.
8. Barber, 'Freiburg'.
9. 'Cycling', Gemeente Utrecht, 26 March 2016, https://www.utrecht.nl/city-of-utrecht/mobility/cycling.
10. Laura Bliss, 'How Utrecht Became a Paradise for Cyclists', Bloomberg UK, 5 July 2019, https://www.bloomberg.com/news/articles/2019-07-05/how-the-dutch-made-utrecht-a-bicycle-first-city.
11. Bliss, 'How Utrecht Became a Paradise for Cyclists'.
12. Renate van der Zee, 'How Amsterdam Became the Bicycle Capital of the World', *Guardian*, 5 May 2015, https://www.theguardian.com/cities/2015/may/05/amsterdam-bicycle-capital-world-transport-cycling-kindermoord.
13. Van der Zee, 'Bicycle Capital of the World'.
14. Roeland Kerbosch, 'Amsterdam Children Fighting Cars in De Pijp', short film, 1972, posted 12 December 2013 by BicycleDutch, YouTube, 9:35, https://youtu.be/YY6PQAI4TZE?si=S_ykxN0Krw_BwTOn.
15. Matthew Bruno, Henk-Jan Dekker and Letícia Lindenberg Lemos, 'Mobility Protests in the Netherlands of the 1970s: Activism, Innovation, and Transitions', *Environmental Innovation and Societal Transitions* 40 (2021): 521–35.
16. Van der Zee, 'Bicycle Capital of the World'.
17. Elliot Fishman, Paul Schepers and Carlijn Barbara Maria Kamphuis, 'Dutch Cycling: Quantifying the Health and Related Economic Benefits', *American Journal of Public Health* 105, no. 8 (2015): e14.
18. Fishman, Schepers and Kamphuis, 'Dutch Cycling', e14.
19. Rachel Aldred, Anna Goodman and James Woodcock, 'Impacts of Active Travel Interventions on Travel Behaviour and Health: Results From a Five-Year Longitudinal Travel Survey in Outer London', *Journal of Transport & Health* 35, no. 1 (2024): 101771, https://doi.org/10.1016/j.jth.2024.101771.
20. Lauren Ghidotti, 'Transforming Paris from Below: Cycling as a Social Movement', Urban Cycling Institute, 11 March 2024, https://urbancyclinginstitute.org/transforming-paris-from-below-cycling-as-a-social-movement.

21. Anne Lehelloco, email to the author, 30 August 2024.
22. Chris Baraniuk, 'The Cities Stripping Out Concrete For Earth and Plants', BBC Future Planet, 23 February 2024, https://www.bbc.co.uk/future/article/20240222-depaving-the-cities-replacing-concrete-with-earth-and-plants.
23. 'National Dutch Championship "Tile-tipping" (NK Tegelwippen)', Interlace Hub, 4 September 2023, https://interlace-hub.com/national-dutch-championship-%E2%80%98tile-tipping%E2%80%99-nk-tegelwippen.
24. See: NK Tegelwippen, https://www.nk-tegelwippen.nl.
25. Thami Croeser et al., 'Finding Space for Nature in Cities: The Considerable Potential of Redundant Car Parking', *npj Urban Sustainability* 2 (2022): 27, https://doi.org/10.1038/s42949-022-00073-x.
26. Croeser et al., 'Finding Space for Nature in Cities', 27.
27. Jo Orchard-Webb, 'Time Rebels in Practice,' CoLab Dudley, Medium, 27 September 2021, https://medium.com/colab-dudley/time-rebels-in-practice-46f62edf038c.
28. 'Cornwall Beaver Project', Cornwall Wildlife Trust, 2 October 2017, https://www.cornwallwildlifetrust.org.uk/what-we-do/our-conservation-work/on-land/beavers/cornwall-beaver-project.
29. Richard E. Brazier et al., 'River Otter Beaver Trial: Science and Evidence Report', https://www.wildlifetrusts.org/sites/default/files/2020-05/River%20Otter%20Beaver%20Trial%20-%20Science%20and%20Evidence%20Report.pdf.
30. Alan Puttock et al., 'Beaver Dams Attenuate Flow: A Multi-Site Study', *Hydrological Processes* 35, no. 2 (2021): e14017, https://doi.org/10.1002/hyp.14017.
31. Benedict MacDonald, *Cornerstone: Wild Forces that can Change Our World* (Bloomsbury, 2022), 60-84.
32. Ruth Williams, 'Where Will England's Next Reservoirs Be?' Utility Week, 1 September 2023, https://utilityweek.co.uk/where-will-englands-next-reservoirs-be.
33. Jacob Dykes, 'The Rightful Return of Beavers to Britain', Geographical, 22 July 2022, https://geographical.co.uk/wildlife/the-return-of-beavers-to-britain.
34. Isobel Cockerell, 'The Secret Movement Bringing Europe's Wildlife Back from the Brink', .coda, 27 June 2023, https://www.codastory.com/waronscience/rewilding-beavers-conservation.
35. 'Coexisting with Beavers', Animal Welfare Institute, 9 May 2022, https://awionline.org/content/coexisting-beavers.
36. Ben Goldfarb, 'Ben Goldfarb on How Beavers Can Boost the Collective Imagination', in conversation with the author, Rob Hopkins, 10 July 2019,

https://www.robhopkins.net/2019/07/10/ben-goldfarb-on-how-beavers-can-boost-the-collective-imagination.

37. Lucy Sherriff, 'The US is Bringing Back Nature's Best Firefighters: Beavers', BBC, 11 January 2024, https://www.bbc.com/future/article/20240111-the-us-is-bringing-back-beavers-because-theyre-natures-best-firefighters.
38. Stella Thompson et al., 'Ecosystem Services Provided by Beavers *Castor* spp.', *Mammal Review* 51, no. 1 (2021): 25–39, https://doi.org/10.1111/mam.12220.
39. Ketan Joshi, '2024 CCS Update: The Revolution Refuses to Arrive', 24 November 2024, https://ketanjoshi.co/2024/11/24/2024-ccs-update-the-revolution-refuses-to-arrive.
40. Dearbail Jordan, 'Water Investors Have Withdrawn Billions, Says Research', BBC News, 10 May 2024, https://www.bbc.co.uk/news/articles/cw4478wnjdpo.
41. Cockerell, 'The Secret Movement'.
42. See: Le Haut-Bois, https://lehautbois.fr.
43. See: Ceinture Aliment-Terre Liégeoise, https://www.catl.be; and CRE@FARM, https://www.liege.be/fr/vivre-a-liege/commerce/alimentation-locale/creafarm. I describe the wider Ceinture Aliment-Terre Liègeoise project in greater detail in my book *From What Is to What If*.
44. Marie-Odile Helme, 'Urbavar has Created a Giant Vegetable Garden for its Employees', Businews, 4 May 2023, https://www.businews.fr/Urbavar-a-cree-un-potager-geant-pour-ses-salaries_a4477.html.
45. A story told in Rob Hopkins, *21 Stories of Transition*, https://transitionnetwork.org/resources/21-stories-of-transition-pdf-to-download or in *Qu'est Ce Qu'on Attend?*, directed by Marie-Monique Robin, produced by David Charrasse (M2R Films, 2016), documentary film, https://m2rfilms.com/qu-est-ce-qu-on-attend.

Chapter 5: Learn from the Pioneers

1. Roman Krznaric, in conversation with the author, 16 April 2024.
2. Mushon Zer-Aviv and Moran, 'Speculative Tourism: Audio Tours from the Future', (undated) Ding, https://dingdingding.org/issue-5/speculative-tourism-audio-tours-from-the-future.
3. Zer-Aviv and Shalev Moran, 'Speculative Tourism'.
4. Mushon Zer-Aviv, in conversation with the author, 28 February 2024.
5. See: Speculative Tourism, https://www.speculativetourism.com.
6. Zer-Aviv, in conversation.
7. 'Town Anywhere', posted 24 February 2024 by Town Anywhere, YouTube, 6:34, https://youtu.be/cRvhY4S94ic?si=mVg0JPzg47FawJnM.

8. 'Town Anywhere - Rehearsing the Future', posted 8 November 2024 by Town Anywhere, YouTube, 4:39, https://youtu.be/0Q4E91c9Xqs?si=e2iWzYLuIkcm8OBd.
9. Harriet Saddington, 'Community-Led Development in Totnes Vows to Fight On: "We Are Determined to Get the Site Back"', The Developer, 29 May 2024, https://www.thedeveloper.live/opinion/community-led-development-in-totnes-vows-to-fight-on-we-are-determined-to-get-the-site-back.
10. 'Brian Eno One-Off Art and Music Action in Support of Atmos Totnes', posted 9 July 2021 by Amos for Totnes, YouTube, 7:09, https://www.youtube.com/watch?v=yHDp1PgewlI.
11. Terran Collective, 'How to Celebrate the "156th Annual" Inheritance Day', Shareable, 2 December 2021, https://www.shareable.net/how-to-celebrate-the-156th-annual-inheritance-day.
12. Terran Collective, 'How to Celebrate'.
13. Tibet Sprague, in conversation with the author, 18 December 2024.
14. Yasmine Tigoé, 'Nantes. Dans la Manif, Un Cosmonaute Venu Du Future', Ouest-France, 18 June 2024, https://www.ouest-france.fr/pays-de-la-loire/nantes-44000/nantes-dans-la-manif-un-cosmonaute-venu-du-futur-2448372c-2d85-11ef-9d8b-818edcab8630.
15. 'Book Walidah Imarisha', Allied Media Projects, updated 26 May 2022, https://alliedmedia.org/post/book-walidah-imarisha.

Chapter 6: Organisations as Time Machines

1. Bannau Brycheiniog National Park, *Dyffodol Y Bannau: The Future*, (Bannau Brycheiniog National Park, 2023), 137, https://future.bannau.wales/introducing-the-management-plan.
2. Bannau Brycheiniog National Park, *Dyffodol Y Bannau: The Future*.
3. Jane Davidson, *#futuregen: Lessons from a Small Country* (Chelsea Green Publishing, 2020).
4. 'M4 Relief Road: Newport Motorway Plans Scrapped', BBC News, 4 June 2019, https://www.bbc.com/news/uk-wales-48512697.
5. See: Moral Imaginations: https://www.moralimaginations.com.
6. Phoebe Tickell and Matt Lloyd-Rose, *Imagination Activism in Camden: Insights From the First Phase* (Moral Imaginations, 2023), https://www.moralimaginations.com/camden-imagines.
7. Hanna Thomas Uose, *The Most Creative Look To The Future: Imagination and Creative Practice in Service of Organizational Transformation* (UN Global Pulse, 2023), https://www.unglobalpulse.org/document/the-most-creative-look-to-the-future-imagination-and-creative-practice-in-service-of-organizational-transformation.
8. Uose, *The Most Creative Look To The Future*, 33.

9. Lauren Parater, in conversation with the author, 9 December 2024.

Chapter 7: Make It Immersive

1. 'Field Recordings from the Future', *Rob Hopkins* (blog), updated 2 February 2024, https://www.robhopkins.net/field-recordings-from-the-future. And yes, is a real person! Mr Kit, https://www.hellomrkit.com/home.
2. William Tullett, *Smell and the Past: Noses, Archives, Narratives* (Bloomsbury Academic, 2023), 3.
3. Laurence Minsky, Colleen Fahey and Caroline Fabregas, 'Inside the Influential World of Scent Branding', *Harvard Business Review*, 11 April 2018, https://hbr.org/2018/04/inside-the-invisible-but-influential-world-of-scent-branding.
4. Susan Magsamen and Ivy Ross, *Your Brain on Art: How the Arts Transform Us* (Canongate, 2023), 4.
5. Hsuan L. Hsu, in conversation with the author, 27 February 2024.
6. Minsky, Fahey and Fabregas, 'Inside the Influential World of Scent Branding'.
7. Minsky, Fahey and Fabregas.
8. Minsky, Fahey and Fabregas.
9. Nissan Europe, 'Nissan Creates "Scent of the Future"', Nissan News, 10 December 2013, https://usa.nissannews.com/en-US/releases/nissan-in-europe-creates-scent-of-the-future?.
10. Nissan Europe, 'Nissan Creates "Scent of the Future"'; 'Nissan Creates "Scent of the Future"', posted 10 December 2013 by Nissan Europe, YouTube, 2:28, https://www.youtube.com/watch?v=BUVuXANIBHw.
11. William Tullett, Smell and the Past: Noses, Archives, Narratives (London: Bloomsbury Academic, 2023) 23.
12. Hsu, in conversation.
13. This is inspired by an activity created by Kirk Hoessle and Steve Van Matre of the Institute for Earth Education, which is called Earthwalks. They describe an Earthwalk as 'a light, refreshing touch of nature that aims to develop the successive feelings of joy, kinship, reverence, and love for this incredible planet we share and its amazing natural systems and communities of life'. See: Steve Van Matre, *Earthwalks: An Alternative Nature Experience* (The Institute for Earth Education, 2019).
14. Rainer Maria Rilke, *Letters to a Young Poet* (Penguin, 2016), 41.
15. Ouassima Laabich, 'On Sensual Futuring', *Ding*, no. 5, 26 June 2018, https://dingdingding.org/issue-5/on-sensual-futuring.
16. Ouassima Laabich, 'Muslim Futures', Superrr, 15 February 2022, https://superrr.net/project/muslimfutures.
17. Ouassima's futures playlist includes 'Night of Arará' by Miki Ikhifa, 'Ruby' by Ali Farka Touré and Toumani Diabaté, 'Bonga' by Mona Ki Ngi Xica,' Jazz

In My Head' by Samthing Soweto, 'As' by Stevie Wonder, 'Sahara Blues' by Majid Bekkas and 'Wahala' by CKay ft. Olamide.

18. Laabich, 'On Sensual Futuring'.
19. Mama D. Ujuaje and Marina Chang, 'Systems of Food and Systems of Violence: An Intervention for the Special Issue on "Community Self Organisation, Sustainability and Resilience in Food Systems"', *Sustainability* 12, no. 17 (2020): 7092, https://doi.org/10.3390/su12177092.
20. Mama D Ujuaje in conversation with the author, 10 January 2025.
21. Rob Hopkins, host, *Cultivating Imagination*, episode 5, 'Activism and Imagination: Rob Hopkins and Michael Datura Discuss Longing, Storytelling, and Fighting for Just Futures', voiceEd Radio Canada, 5 March 2024, 52:40, https://www.spreaker.com/episode/ep-5-activism-and-imagination-rob-hopkins-and-michael-datura-discuss-longing-storytelling-and-fighting-for-just-futures--58936785.
22. Michael Datura, email to the author, 31 January 2025.
23. 'Citizen science broadly refers to the active engagement of the general public in scientific research tasks. Citizen science is a growing practice in which scientists and citizens collaborate to produce new knowledge for science and society. Althoughcitizen science has been around for centuries, the term citizen science was coined in the 1990s and has gained popularity since then. Recognition of citizen science is growing in the fields of science, policy, and education and in wider society. It is establishing itself as a field of research and a field of practice, increasing the need for overarching insights, standards, vocabulary, and guidelines.' Katrin Vohland et al., 'Editorial: The Science of Citizen Science Evolves', in *The Science of Citizen Science*, eds. Katrin Vohland et al. (Springer, 2021), 1–12, https://doi.org/10.1007/978-3-030-58278-4_1.
24. 'Cortes Island Academy Showcase: A Journey to 2040', Campbell River School District 72, 29 January 2025, https://www.sd72.bc.ca/_ci/p/19664.
25. An activity described in Joanna Macy and Molly Young Brown, *Coming Back to Life: Practices to Reconnect Our Lives, Our World* (New Society Publishers, 1998).
26. Datura, email.
27. Datura.

Chapter 8: Tell a New Story of Time

1. Barbara Adam, *Time* (Polity Press, 2004), 136.
2. Cecil Rhodes, *The Last Will and Testament of Cecil John Rhodes*, ed. W.T. Steed (Review of Review Office, 1902), 190.
3. Lord Rosebery, quoted in Stephen Kern, *The Culture of Space and Time 1880–1918* (Harvard University Press, 1983), 93–94.

4. adrienne maree brown, *Emergent Strategy: Shaping Change, Changing Worlds* (AK Press, 2017), 21.
5. Fred Polak, *The Image of the Future* (Elsevier Scientific Publishing Company, 1973), 7.
6. 'Temporal Fluidity', Fiveable, https://library.fiveable.me/key-terms/performance-art/temporal-fluidity.
7. Rasni L. Stanford, 'Remembering the Future in North Philadelphia: Engaging Community Futurisms to Restore Hope and Healing in the Face of Collective Trauma', in *Black Quantum Futurism: Space-Time Collapse II: Community Futurisms*, ed. Rasheedah Phillips (The Afrofuturist Affair / House of Future Sciences Books, 2020), 61.
8. Rasheedah Phillips, 'Organise Your Own Temporality: Notes on Self-Determined Temporalities and Radical Futurities', in *We Travel the Spaceways: Black Imagination, Fragments and Diffractions*, eds. Henriette Gunkel and Kara Lynch (Verlag, 2019), 237.
9. Roy Christopher, 'Preface', in *Boogie Down Productions: Hip Hop, Time and Afrofuturism*, ed. Ray Christopher (Strange Attractor Press, 2022), 13.
10. Clara Herrmann, 'In Conversation with Rasheedah Phillips: Black Futurism & Technologies of Joy', Contemporary And, 9 June 2020, https://contemporaryand.com/magazines/black-futurism-technologies-of-joy.
11. Herrmann, 'In Conversation with Rasheedah Phillips'.
12. Dana Rice, 'Black Designers Demand Equity and Justice in the Built Environment', Hidden City, 31 August 2020, https://hiddencityphila.org/2020/08/black-designers-demand-equity-and-justice-in-the-built-environment; Quoted in Michael McCanne, 'Time Travellers: Black Quantum Futurism in Philadephia', Art in America, 3 November 2016, https://www.artnews.com/art-in-america/features/time-travelers-black-quantum-futurism-in-philadelphia-60021.
13. Michael McCanne, 'Time Travellers: Black Quantum Futurism in Philadephia', Art in America, 3 November 2016, https://www.artnews.com/art-in-america/features/time-travelers-black-quantum-futurism-in-philadelphia-60021.
14. Rasheedah Phillips, 'Communal, Quantum and Afrofutures: Time and Memory in North Philly', in *Black Quantum Futurism: Space-Time Collapse II: Community Futurisms,* ed. Rasheedah Phillips (The Afrofuturist Affair / House of Future Sciences Books, 2020); Also, a beautiful short film gives a sense of how the Community Futures Labs worked: 'Collectively Envisioning a Future for North Philadelphia', Black Quantum Futurism (A Blade of Grass, 2018), short film, https://vimeo.com/296902589?share=copy.

15. Rasheedah Phillips ed., *Black Quantum Futurism: Space-Time Collapse II: Community Futurisms* (The Afrofuturist Affair / House of Future Sciences Books, 2020), 191.
16. 'Time Camp 001', Black Quantum Futurism, 1 October 2017, https://www.blackquantumfuturism.com/time-camp-001.
17. Ana Prendes, 'Black Quantum Futurism: "Black Diasporan Temporalities Share Many Parallels with Quantum Principles"', Arts at CERN, 26 March 2021, https://arts.cern/black-quantum-futurisms-cpt-reversal-features-the-first-artworks-from-their-residency-at-cern.
18. Text for both these documents taken from images of Afronautic Research Labs performance: malstad, 'Afronautic Research Lab', Flickr, 10 February 2016, https://www.flickr.com/photos/factoryfarm/with/50442284977.
19. Camille Turner, 'An Afronautic Journey', artist talk, posted 10 July 2023 by Library of Infinities, YouTube, 29:41, https://www.youtube.com/watch?v=Kjtq9W4prvY.
20. 'Bio', Camille Turner, https://www.camilleturner.com/bio-cv.
21. Camille Turner, 'Unsilencing the Past: Staging Black Atlantic Memory in Canada and Beyond.' (PhD dissertation, York University, 2022).
22. If you're wondering whether I spelled 'deeep' wrong back there, I didn't – it's intentional. As Promona explains, 'The crew decided to spell the adjective with an extra "e," to nominally point towards the ridiculousness inherent in attempts at comprehension. Deeep is also a word that makes your mouth stretch more than necessary; signaling a pleasurable broadening of horizons.'; Promona Sengupta, 'Ammunitions: Time Travel as Survival', BAK, 21 April 2022, https://bakonline.org/en/research+publications/prospections/iridescent+ammunitions+time+travel+as+survival.
23. Promona Sengupta, 'A Guide to the Visceral Science of Time Travel,' *Ding*, no. 5, 26 June 2018, https://dingdingding.org/issue-5/a-guide-to-the-visceral-science-of-time-travel.
24. Sengupta, 'A Guide to the Visceral Science of Time Travel'; Promona Sengupta, 'Time Travel for All: How to Leave No One Behind', posted 27 August 2021 by DYCA, YouTube, 29:54, https://www.youtube.com/watch?v=cLLJnlMaLsg.
25. Sengupta, 'A Guide to the Visceral Science of Time Travel'.
26. FLINTAQ+ is a term that stands for Female, Lesbian, Intersex, Non-binary, Trans, Agender People and Queer People.
27. Sengupta, 'A Guide to the Visceral Science of Time Travel'.
28. Stephen Kern, *The Culture of Space and Time 1880-1918* (Harvard University Press, 1983), 11.
29. This quote has been attributed to everyone from Albert Einstein to Mark Twain, but initially appeared in March 1919 in a story called 'The Girl in

the Golden Atom' by Ray Cummings, which was published in a magazine called *All-Story Weekly*. The story of how that quote then spread can be found here: 'Quote Origin: Time Is What Keeps Everything From Happening At Once', Quote Investigator, 6 July 2019, https://quoteinvestigator.com/2019/07/06/time.

30. Robert E. Ornstein, *On the Experience of Time* (Penguin Books, 1969), 101.
31. Ornstein, *On the Experience of Time*, 109.
32. Emmanuel Vaughan-Lee, 'Another Kind of Time: An Interview with Jenny Odell', *Emergence Magazine*, 26 April 2023, https://emergencemagazine.org/interview/another-kind-of-time.
33. John S. Mbiti, *African Religions and Philosophy* (Heinemann, 1975), 17.
34. Mbiti, *African Religions and Philosophy*, 17.
35. Jonathan Alabi, 'A Critical Assessment of J.S. Mbiti's African Conception of Time' (n.d.), https://www.academia.edu/83089708/A_CRITICAL_ASSESSMENT_OF_J_S_MBITIS_AFRICAN_CONCEPTION_OF_TIME.
36. Rev. Fr. Joseph T. Ekong, 'Rethinking John S. Mbiti's Metaphysical Trajectory of Time in Africa', *European Journal of Philosophy, Culture and Religious Studies* 6, no.1 (2022): 54.
37. Alabi, 'A Critical Assessment'.
38. Mbiti, *African Religions and Philosophy*, 23.
39. Giordano Nanni, *The Colonisation of Time: Ritual, Routine and Resistance in the British Empire* (Manchester University Press, 2012), 29.
40. Nanni, *The Colonisation of Time*, 59.
41. James Gleick, *Time Travel: A History* (Pantheon Books, 2016), 86.
42. Kern, *The Culture of Space and Time 1880-1918*, 12.
43. Nanni, *The Colonisation of Time*, 1.
44. Maureen Perkins, *The Reform of Time: Magic and Modernity* (Pluto Press, 2001), 84.
45. Walter Johnson, 'Possible Pasts: Some Speculations on Time, Temporality and the History of Atlantic Slavery', *American Studies* 45, no. 4 (2000): 490.
46. Laura M. Giurge, Ashley V. Whillans and Colin West, 'Why Time Poverty Matters for Individuals, Organisations and Nations', *Nature Human Behaviour* 4 (2020): 993.
47. Giurge, Whillans and West, 'Why Time Poverty Matters', 999.

Chapter 9: From the Impossible to the Not Yet

1. Namwali Serpell, 'The Zambian "Afronaut" Who Wanted To Join the Space Race', *New Yorker*, 11 March 2017, https://www.newyorker.com/culture/culture-desk/the-zambian-afronaut-who-wanted-to-join-the-space-race.

2. 'Zambia's Forgotten Space Program', Lusaka Times, 28 January 2011, https://www.lusakatimes.com/2011/01/28/space-program.
3. Serpell, 'The Zambian "Afronaut"'.
4. 'Zambia's Forgotten Space Program', Lusaka Times.
5. Brent Hayes Edwards, 'The Race for Space: Sun Ra's poetry', in Sun Ra: *The Immeasurable Equation*, eds. James L. Wolf and Harmut Geerken (Waitawhile, 2005), 33.
6. Audrey Thomas McCluskey, '"We Specialise in the Wholly Impossible": Black Women School Founders and Their Mission', Signs 22, no.2 (1997): 403, https://doi.org/10.1086/495166.
7. Slavoj Žižek, *Demanding the Impossible*, ed. Yong-june Park (Polity Press, 2013), 143–144.
8. Peter H. Marshall, *Demanding the Impossible: A History of Anarchism* (The Anarchist Library, 1993), 7.
9. I won't go into Sun Ra's whole life story here, for that I highly recommend John F. Szwed, *Space is the Place: The Lives and Times of Sun Ra* (Mojo Books, 2000).
10. William Sites, '"We Travel the Spaceways": Urban Utopianism and the Imagined Spaces of Black Experimental Music', *Urban Geography* 33, no. 4, (2012): 585, https://doi.org/10.2747/0272-3638.33.4.566.
11. William Sites, *Sun Ra's Chicago: Afrofuturism and the City* (University of Chicago Press, 2020), 165.
12. Roger Quail, 'Gig 64. Sun Ra, The Octagon Centre, Sheffield University, 15th October 1983', *My Life in the Mosh of Ghosts* (blog), 16 April 2024, April 16, 2024, https://www.mylifeinthemoshofghosts.com/2024/04/16/gig-64-sun-ra-the-octagon-centre-sheffield-university-15th-october-1983.
13. Sites, '"We Travel the Spaceways"', 568–69.
14. Ben Anderson, "A Principle of Hope: Recorded Music, Listening Practices and the Immanence of Utopia', *Geografiska Annaler: Series B, Human Geography* 84, no. 3–4 (2002): 218, https://doi.org/10.1111/j.0435-3684.2002.00125.x.
15. William Sites, in conversation with the author, 12 January 2022.
16. Marina McDougall, in conversation with the author, 3 June 2024.
17. 'Summoning the Future Forest with the Sun Ra Arkestra', S(tree)twork, https://streetworkproject.net/intra-galactic-forest.
18. You can see a video record of this evening at: https://youtu.be/_xN6z3HGeYc?si=ijBblVENaHBxkJKk.
19. 'Second Sun' by Bonobo is especially good 'stepping into the future and taking a walk around' music in my experience. Thanks to Ruth Ben-Tovim for pointing out its possibilities.

20. Elise Boulding, 'A Journey into the Future: Imagining a Nonviolent World', *Peace and Conflict Studies* 9, no. 1 (2002): 54.
21. Peter Andre et al., 'Globally Representative Evidence on the Actual and Perceived Support for Climate Action', *Nature Climate Change* 14 (2024): 253, https://doi.org/10.1038/s41558-024-01925-3.
22. Andreas Arp, 'Den danske oliejagt har brudt med centrale miljøregler i 34 år: Kan føre til stop for olieproduktionen', 14 September 2024, Altinget, https://www.altinget.dk/artikel/den-danske-oliejagt-har-brudt-med-centrale-miljoeregler-i-34-aar-kan-foere-til-stop-for-olieproduktionen.
23. Federica Bedendo and Evie Lake, 'Coal Mine Plan Quashed by High Court', 13 September 2024, BBC News, https://www.bbc.com/news/articles/cdrlrkz5k2ro.
24. Bedendo and Lake, 'Coal Mine Plan Quashed'.

Chapter 10: A Time Machine Blueprint

1. You can download this file at: https://on.soundcloud.com/PJEy5SUywc9kH7KA8. Feel free to use it, just crediting where it comes from.
2. Sinead Butler, 'Teacher Goes Viral After Using Assassin's Creed to Teach History', indy100, 3 February 2024, https://www.indy100.com/tiktok/teacher-assassins-creed-history-lesson-tiktok.
3. Food waste campaign organisation Feedback have done this before. They call it 'Feeding the Five Thousand': https://feedbackglobal.org/campaigns/feeding-the-5000.
4. Inspired by Sun Ra's 'Outer Space Employment Agency' in the film *Space is the Place*.
5. Luigi Vitali, 'Editor's Letter: Uncancelling the Future', *Dust*, Winter/Spring 2025, 26–27.
6. This already happens in Munich, Germany. See: Benjamin David, 'Experience: I Swim to Work', *Guardian*, 29 September 2017, https://www.theguardian.com/lifeandstyle/2017/sep/29/experience-i-swim-to-work.
7. Anthea Lawson (@anthlawson1), 'Am noticing there's lots of people that @ExtinctionR woke up to taking action on #climate who are currently marking time', X, 12 January 2022, https://x.com/anthlawson1/status/1481285170950979601.
8. T.J. Demos, *Radical Futurisms: Ecologies of Collapse, Chronopolitics, and Justice-to-Come* (Sternberg Press, 2023), 41.

Afterword

1. Angela Carter, *The Infernal Desire Machines of Doctor Hoffman* (Penguin Books, 2010), 12.

2. Carter, *The Infernal Desire Machines*, 17.
3. The Atlantic Meridional Overturning Circulation (AMOC) is a system of ocean currents in the Atlantic Ocean that plays a crucial role in maintaining the balance of the global climate by moving heat and nutrients around the world; Jay A. Baker et al., 'Continued Atlantic Overturning Circulation Even Under Climate Extremes', *Nature* 638 (2025): 987–94, https://doi.org/10.1038/s41586-024-08544-0.
4. There are already people who work in advertising who get the scale of the challenge and are committed to using their 'dark arts' for good. See: Purpose Disruptors, https://www.purposedisruptors.org.
5. See: Sophie Mess, https://www.sophiemess.com; ATM, https://atmstreetart.com; Mona Caron, https://monacaron.com.

Index

Index

Index

Index

Index

About the Author

Arlo Hopkins

Rob Hopkins is a co-founder of Transition Town Totnes and Transition Network, and the author of *The Transition Handbook*, *The Transition Companion*, *The Power of Just Doing Stuff*, *21 Stories of Transition* and, most recently, *From What Is to What If: Unleashing the Power of Imagination to Create the Future We Want*. He has also collaborated with artist Mr Kit on the music project Field Recordings from the Future.

He presented 100 episodes of the podcast series *From What If to What Next*. In 2012, he was voted one of the *Independent*'s top 100 environmentalists and was on Nesta and the *Observer*'s list of Britain's 50 New Radicals. Hopkins has also appeared on BBC Radio 4's *Four Thought* and *A Good Read*, in the French film phenomenon *Demain* and its sequel, *Apres Demain*, and has spoken at TEDGlobal and three TEDx events.

An Ashoka Fellow, Hopkins also holds a doctorate degree from the University of Plymouth and has received two honorary doctorates from the University of the West of England and the University of Namur. In November 2022, he was made an Honorary Citizen of Liège in Belgium by the mayor of the city. He has run his 'How to Fall in Love with the Future' training sessions with organisations across Europe. He is a keen gardener, drypoint etching printmaker and artist. He blogs at robhopkins.net where you can also subscribe to his monthly newsletter, *The Time Traveller's Gazette*.